BOLD
SCHOOL
BRAND

Foreword by Dr Ian PM Lambert

How to leverage brand strategy to reposition, differentiate, and market your school

Brad Entwistle, Josh Miles and Andrew Sculthorpe

Published by imageseven, Perth, Australia.

The material in this publication is of the nature of general comment only and does not represent professional advice. It is not intended to provide specific guidance for particular circumstances, and it should not be relied on as the basis for any decision to take action or not take action on any matter which it covers. Readers should obtain professional advice, where appropriate, before making any such decision. To the maximum extent permitted by law, the authors and publishers disclaim all responsibility and liability to any person arising directly or indirectly from any person taking or not taking action based on the information in this publication.

ISBN 978-0-6485596-0-3

Printed in Australia.

To all school Heads, who take on one of the toughest jobs on earth,
aiming to build a better world. Thank you for allowing us to partner with you.

To the imageseven team, without this great group of people none of these ideas or
concepts would have been brought to life. Always a privilege to work with you.

Contents

Foreword

Introduction

Section I
Brand strategy

Section II
Brand voice

Section III
Brand identity

Section V
Brand culture

Section VI
Bonus content

Why exactly are we here?

Foreword

When someone thinks of your school, *what* do they think? That is your brand. Every school has one.

In years past, schools have been less confident in articulating their deeply held missional beliefs and values. Most schools have not considered their brand to be an integral part of executing their mission, but times have changed. Schools can no longer rely on reputation spread by word of mouth alone. To thrive into the future, Heads need to proactively manage their school's brand.

The book you now hold in your hands is the first framework designed specifically to help school Heads build their school's brand. Having a Bold School Brand is important because, if you do it well, it allows you to take all that complexity and position your school very clearly and succinctly to your internal community, as well as to prospective parents. So, developing a Bold School Brand is about making the complex simple, but not making it superficial.

I have worked with the team at imageseven since 1998. I have witnessed firsthand their quest to take rapidly evolving best practices from the commercial sector and adapt them into a branding framework that is tested and optimised for schools. This framework is not a generic business concept with an educational veneer. The Bold School Brand framework has been built from the ground up specifically to assist Heads lift their school brands and help them achieve their mission.

To educate students well is to leave a legacy for the future. It is about providing young men and women with a pathway into that future — where they will build good relationships with their families, invent great things, and solve great problems. If schools were made up of educators alone, we would not get the job done. We need the help and guidance of skilled professionals who have that burning desire to take us places we could never think of, to consistently hone our message, and to join us on our mission. It is important work and we are in it together.

Dr Ian PM Lambert
Principal
The Scots College, Sydney

Where are all the school brands?

A brief history of school marketing and why the old ways are no longer enough.

Historically speaking, marketing activity for schools can be summed up in one word: Relationships. However, market changes mean this is no longer enough. With the model changing, why are so many schools resisting new ways of building their brands and marketing themselves?

Why school brands need help

According to the Independent Schools Council of Australia, there are more than 1,140 independent schools in Australia. These schools are among the most sought-after in the world. And, until recent years, having a large ad in the phone book, networking alumni connections, and a brochure-style website were the only types of marketing activities these schools needed to do.

While most schools have been sticking with the basics, a marketing revolution has been taking place. Companies have been spending billions of dollars worldwide to market their business to consumer (B2C) and business to business (B2B) products and services. The goal? To create and leverage unique and memorable brands in an increasingly crowded marketplace.

Today, school marketers are realising they need to join the revolution.

With the prevalence of web-based technologies and social media, schools are joining B2C and B2B companies in doing more and more business online.

But when we look at social media, that's different to branding or marketing, right? Where does one end and the other begin, especially in the context of a school?

Brand is the sum of everything your school is

In his groundbreaking book, *The Brand Gap: How to Bridge the Distance Between Business Strategy and Design*, Marty Neumeier defines brand as "the sum of everything you are."

Neumeier says your brand is "not what *you* say it is, it's what *they* say it is." His overarching argument is that a chasm exists between logic and magic in most organisations. He suggests that a greater focus on brand could close that gap and generate even greater success.

We couldn't agree more.

At imageseven, we define brand as: "Who you are, what you promise, and your ability and willingness to keep that promise. "It's a simple premise, isn't it?

Yet we have education clients with years of marketing or design experience who remain fuzzy on how to grow or influence the development of their school's brand. Somehow the idea that "it's what they say it is" feels like a reason not to try to improve the brand. If the brand is created only in people's minds, somehow the very exercise of branding seems like trickery — intentionally trying to mislead stakeholders such as parents, staff, and students.

We believe your brand encompasses every element of your school. It's in how you deliver your educational product or service, your buildings, your visual identity, your use of language, and everything from an email signature to sounds and images on your website. Just as importantly, it's in your student and parent experiences, policies, service levels, and the conversations being had about your school. In short, it's everything from your school's physical existence to its reputation.

So if brand is everything that surrounds your school, what good is branding?

It's important to remember that much of a brand is passive. We can't possibly control or influence the conversations teachers and support staff have about our school on the weekends, or the reputation we have for poor customer service, right? Wrong. Branding certainly can't take a lousy school and help it look like a great one. However, focusing on what needs improvement from the ground up and the inside out, and repackaging the school in a new light, can successfully and completely recreate the public image of its brand. That's why they call it a rebrand.

Your school's brand is like a living, breathing, malleable and pliable entity. It's greatly influenced by intentional positioning and differentiation but is also responsive to the feedback of your staff, parents and students. It's what allows you to charge a premium for the same education services your competition offers.

Brand is what keeps your school not only top of mind in the marketplace, but also preferred.

Why are schools so far behind?

As world-renowned sales trainer Zig Ziglar once said: "People buy from people." So if branding products and services is a worthy endeavour, why has the education sector been so overlooked by marketers, branding, and design companies?

We have two theories.

The first is that working for better-known B2C clients such as consumer packaged goods, vehicle manufacturers, and sports franchises seems more exciting than schools.

The second is that school Heads — and often the marketers who try to serve them — don't know where to begin.

Developing a unique brand for a school is a collaborative effort, often between multiple stakeholders, and schools conform to an academic culture and norms. 'Selling' their institution doesn't come naturally. Building a great brand from these conditions is no simple task. That's why in today's marketplace, you are more likely to find educational 'bland brands' — a collection of undifferentiated, me-too school brands that do things the way they always have.

Where can we find evidence of these school bland brands? An obvious place to start is the internet. Most schools rely on their website or social media presence to take care of their branding needs. Unfortunately, the roots of their marketing problems are not in the quality of either. They're in the absence of an overarching, holistic brand strategy and a failure to find, leverage, and express the most distinguishing elements of their brand.

It's time to ditch your bland brand and create a Bold School Brand.

Bold School Brand is a framework and best practice approach designed to help schools identify a niche, position themselves within that niche, and build a compelling brand. This framework guides them step-by-step through the process, illuminating potential pitfalls along the way.

As varied as schools may be, why would they all benefit from operating from the same branding framework?

It's as simple as knowing where to begin, what to build from, and which elements of your branding and marketing can and should evolve over time. In today's online marketplace, even brilliant marketers can quickly waste energy and resources on the wrong tactics at the wrong times. As new social networks, mobile technologies, cloud-based apps and other new media emerge as the latest and greatest marketing channels, even the most experienced marketers wonder if these approaches are where their marketing dollars should be spent today, if at all.

Behind closed doors: The questions about brands

When talking with school Heads and marketing professionals, we hear the same problems and concerns over and over. We've been questioned about the permanence of social media. Listened to stories about the challenges of standing out in a crowded marketplace. Been regaled by tales of schools growing out of control, with no consistent way of sharing their culture with new staff. And we've heard the frustration of bringing an unmatched education offering to market, only to have to compete on price against dozens of lesser qualified, me-too schools.

The most interesting questions are the ones we hear behind closed doors — the whispered questions that people ask once we've developed a deeper level of trust. These are the types of things we hear nearly every week:

"Branding? Marketing? Website? How do we know what to tackle first? All I know is that we need to drive enrolments."

"We're an outstanding school, but we're always competing against these lower-tier competitors. Nobody seems to understand that comparing us to other schools just isn't comparing apples to apples. So often the decision comes down to which is the cheapest. How do we convince parents we're the best school for their child?"

"Sure, I think strategy is important, but isn't social media what everyone else is focusing on right now?"

"I may have marketing in my title, but I don't know anything about that creative stuff. That's why we need you guys. Does that stuff really work?"

"We don't need branding. We already have a brand. All our parents know who we are, and all our enrolments are from our relationships."

"I don't know the difference between marketing and advertising. Should we budget for them separately?"

"I don't think we're going to do any branding ads. We've tried that before and they're a waste of money."

"My niece designed our logo (*gesturing to the sign on the wall*). It's a little difficult to reproduce in colour, but we don't want to change it anytime soon. She'd be devastated."

"We spent a lot of money on that sign out front. It's just not worth rebranding if we have to replace it. Signs are expensive."

"All we need is to make our website look more up-to-date. We can give you the stock photos and the shot of our building. We'll show you where to put everything. That should be pretty straightforward, right?"

"We can address our brand strategy later. For now, we have to get more enrolment leads through our website."

"Okay, you've been talking a lot through this process about branding. What exactly do you mean by this whole brand thing?"

Do any of these questions sound familiar? As mentioned earlier, they're very common. In fact, in the education space, this disconnect between the power of a brand and its connection to the bottom line is pretty much the rule.

Not all the people asking these questions are in a marketing position as such. Often, they are school leaders. Few have much experience in building a brand, let alone any formal training in design, branding, or marketing. Sometimes, the people who do have marketing training are even more difficult to deal with. Many understand the formal definitions but lack the real-world experience of actually doing marketing. So from our perspective, there's a great deal of confusion and apprehension when it comes to tackling branding and marketing issues in schools across the board.

While branding is at its heart a creative process, for many school Heads it often sounds too soft and nebulous to have any tangible value.

Nothing could be further from the truth. In this book, we'll walk you through a proven process that shows how to find your school's niche, position it, and develop a Bold School Brand.

Occasionally, we'll use brand examples from the world of business to illustrate a concept or execution. This is because there are few global or national school brands that all readers will recognise and we would have to keep explaining the context, which isn't the best use of your time. So instead, we've gone with brand examples from the commercial world that will probably be familiar to most of you — the lessons are the same.

Brand strategy

> Strategy doesn't have to be a complicated subject. It's just a way to get your team singing from the same songbook. A good strategy clearly defines the problem, takes into account all the variables, and provides guidance in the form of a plan of action. In this section of the book, we investigate the roots of brand strategy, how to define your goals and objectives, and make recommendations for positioning and differentiating your school.

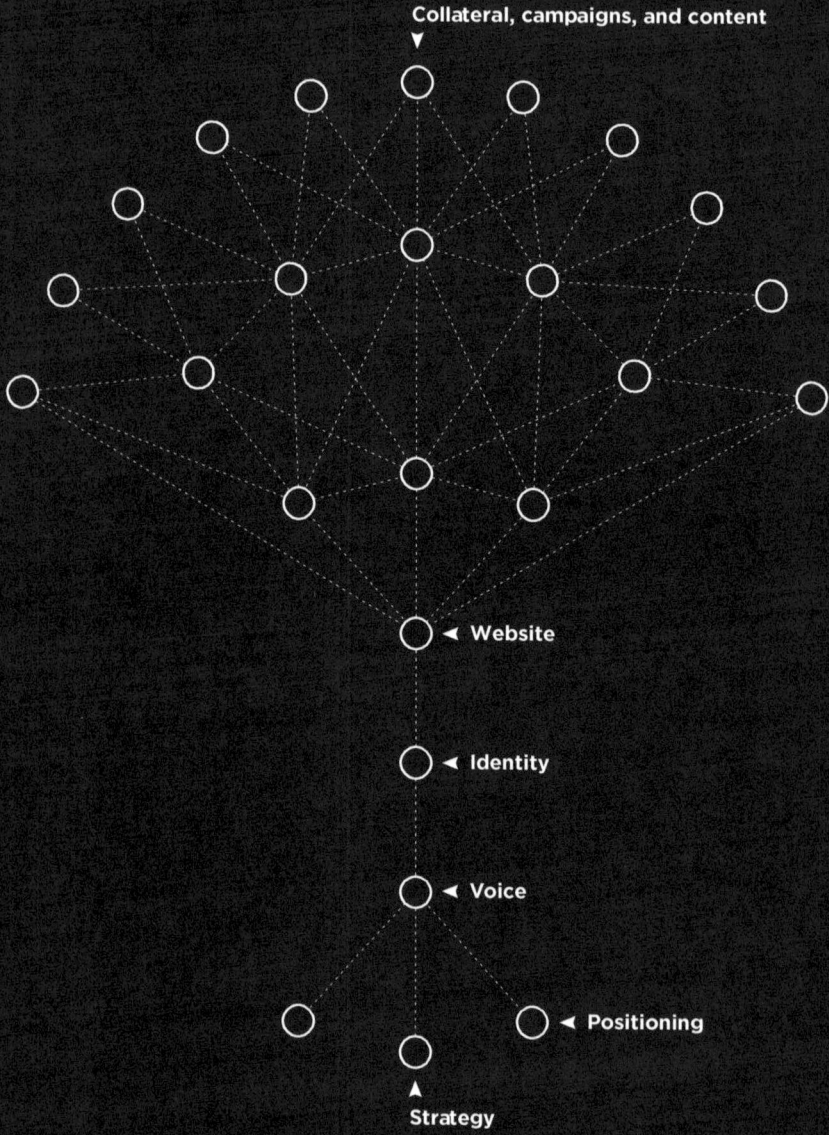

Collateral, campaigns, and content

Website

Identity

Voice

Positioning

Strategy

CHAPTER ONE

The roots of brand strategy

Why you need a brand strategy for your school and where you should start.

Regardless of a school's size, developing a strong strategy is the most important starting point for any branding exercise. It's also the most common step in the process to meet resistance.

Why is that?

Two problems in the marketing industry today create this strategy phobia.

The first problem: Creative firms allow clients to skip out on brand strategy.

How many times have you considered a branding exercise where the only deliverable was a logo, with no strategic rationale involved? Doesn't this seem counterintuitive? Why would a creative firm that's supposedly focused on building your school's brand allow you to skimp on strategy?

The reality is most creative firms are more interested in creating the pretty, shiny deliverables (the graphic elements) and are happy to crank out another design. Later, they will blame the client for 'not getting it' and say, "what a shame they don't value our process."

In the medical world, when a physician operates on a patient before performing a thorough diagnostic, it's called malpractice. Selling a logo without any strategy to back it up is marketing malpractice. This type of negligence creates a bad name for designers, marketers and branding firms everywhere. It causes well-intentioned clients to believe that branding is a waste of money or, even worse, that branding doesn't work.

The second problem: Strategy sounds difficult and unattainable.

Strategy can appear very self-important and complex when it's wrapped up in marketing jargon. However, it is simply a word that means 'plan of action'.

Telling your brand story

What can we learn about branding from trees?

Before you can fully develop an action plan, you need to know where you're starting from and where you want to go. Your brand strategy is that plan. Think of it as the bottom layer of the brand pyramid from which everything else grows, just as a tree grows from its roots.

From its beginnings as a seed, the DNA of the tree tells it exactly what it was designed to do, where it needs to grow, and how to thrive in its environment. When the seed comes to rest in the right spot, it begins to take root. It digs deep with an ever-expanding root system and reaches out to the sky with green, growing branches. As the young sapling feeds, it becomes the centre of its own ecosystem.

Specific types of trees are easy to identify. They offer clues about what family they are from, what their use may be, and what kinds of animals might interact with them.

Different kinds of trees exist in distinct environments. They weather heat, rain, and extreme conditions. But no matter how mighty the tree, even the tiniest invader can spell the end.

Mighty trees also occasionally need maintenance. Whether it's nature's pruning through a windstorm, an animal's occasional snack, or the master gardener's discerning touch, trees may be cultivated to grow perfectly for their intended site, or twist and turn into a distorted existence. Pruning alone is not enough to encourage a tree to thrive in a location that isn't ideal for it.

Landscape designers must take into account the tree's dimensions and growing time. A small tree may fit perfectly into a space today, but in 30 years will that location still best serve the tree and its surroundings?

Even novice gardeners understand the basics. When you plant a hardy tree in fertile ground and allow for plenty of sunshine and water, the result will be a healthy tree with a long, bright future. Other times it's not that simple. You may know you want to grow a tree but understand that your environment is challenging. You may need a landscaping expert to provide guidance so your tree can thrive.

What about a gnarled tree that's aging and in bad shape? Well, unfortunately for the tree, it cannot decide one day to pursue a new strategy to become a majestic redwood.

A brand, on the other hand (with a lot of work and focus on the right things in the right order), can overcome what and where it has been in the past.

Taking the time to consider each element of your brand will help shape it into what you know it can be: A brand that will be easily recognised and well-known. A brand that can be the centre of its own ecosystem. A brand that can grow, adapt, and thrive with the seasons. And a brand that is easily differentiated from the rest of the brands in the forest.

It's true that the kind of holistic branding exercise we're advocating does require input from all your school's stakeholders. Every party involved (school Head, teachers, support staff, parents, students, and your communications and marketing team) must commit time to it.

But it isn't hard, especially using the step-by-step DRIVE qualitative research and brand strategy development process we've developed at imageseven. Based on our signature communication and marketing strategy development tools, it will help you create a robust and comprehensive Bold School Brand strategy.

Let's go for a DRIVE

DRIVE stands for Discovery, Research, Insights, brand Voice, and brand Essence.

Discovery

Discovery is all about learning from our clients and seeing the world from their point of view — from the inside out. We meet with all internal stakeholders so we can better understand the school's goals, perceptions, and concerns. This usually involves extensive consultation in the form of a discovery meeting and interviews with the school's leaders, educators, student body, parents, and even alumni. There might also be a series of exercises with the internal or external marketing team to envision the school's future state, and find out which initiatives are the most advanced and which are the most hollow.

Research

Research is our attempt to flip the lens around to see how the world sees our clients — from the outside in. We survey parents, interview alumni, review competitors, and perform a brand audit. This generally involves reviewing anything and everything the school touches, whether it's the website, signage, on-hold messaging, open days, or brochures. See 'Performing a brand audit' on the following page.

Insights

Once we've gathered opinions and done qualitative research, we compile our thoughts, findings, and recommendations for moving forward. These insights may include a recommended brand architecture, positioning ideas, or a SWOT analysis that pinpoints the strengths, weaknesses, opportunities, and threats to the school's brand. When we present this information, we start to see Heads nodding around the room, but it's also an opportunity to make adjustments if there's anything we've misunderstood or where we've failed to get the phrasing just right for the stakeholders. Sometimes changing one or two words makes all the difference between being rejected and resonating with the audience.

Voice

We'll spend more time describing brand voice in chapter six, so here's the short version: It's all about the tone and how your brand sounds across written communications and messaging. We typically present a few headlines and longer-form paragraphs, coupled with mood boards implying where the school could go with the visual design in the future.

Essence

We'll talk about brand essence in chapter four. The brand essence in your process should probably precede developing a brand voice, but we present voice and essence together, with the brand essence as the capstone to our brand strategy process.

Performing a brand audit

This is a key step in the process, so we'll describe it in more detail.

For a new school, it probably isn't necessary as there won't be much to audit. However, if you've been an established institution for several years, you may be surprised at the clues your past marketing efforts can provide for carving out your future Bold School Brand.

Who should perform the brand audit? Every school is different, so there is no 'one size fits all' approach. Regardless of whether you assemble an in-house team or hire an outside consultant or agency, you need one very important thing — an honest objectivity.

An extensive brand audit should look at most of the following categories.

Internal:
- Positioning
- Brand values
- Unique selling proposition (USP), brand promise, or brand essence
- Voice
- Culture
- Market positioning.

External:
- Brand identity — logos, corporate colours, typefaces, and other brand elements
- Collateral — brochures, print materials, expo displays, etc.
- Advertising
- Website
- Search Engine Optimisation (SEO)
- Social media
- Sponsorships/civic involvement/memberships
- News/Public Relations (PR)
- Content marketing and other assets — blogs, white papers, case studies, articles, books, etc.
- Testimonials
- Videos.

Systems:
- Brand identity/standards
- Human Resources (HR) policies/onboarding process
- Enrolment process/touchpoints
- Internal systems
- Customer service systems.

Brand audit: Before and after

In today's increasingly complex market, there is a hyper-focus (and rightfully so) on return on investment (ROI). Of course, ROI isn't just a tactic to keep the bean counters satisfied — weighing the financial benefits of your branding decisions throughout the process will help guide difficult decisions.

One way you can demonstrate ROI is by conducting a brand audit before and after a rebrand. This will show where the branding exercise helped improve systems and close gaps.

Want to begin a brand audit on your own? See Section VI for your DIY Bold School Brand audit.

It's important to do the maths. How many new enrolments would you have to win to justify the cost of a rebrand? For many schools, one or two new enrolments a year would be more than enough to justify the investment.

Linking strategy to action

The imageseven 'strategy first' methodology for creating brand strategy has been executed in more than 50 schools and refined over 15 years.

The brand strategy that results should be the basis of all your marketing efforts. Many people use the term 'marketing strategy' when what they're really talking about is marketing tactics. However, if you don't have a larger strategy as a guide, you're just going to be guessing about the tactics you should be using as part of your marketing efforts. It provides the long-term guidance that ensures success despite the inevitable ups, downs, and pressures across the school year.

During DRIVE we find, name, and identify your school's top strategic priorities. Many tactics are probably strategically correct (or at least not incorrect), but our focus is on identifying the 'strategic elephants' — the ten or twenty percent improvement opportunities — rather than the tactics that will deliver just one or two percent improvement.

The DRIVE process has three significant outputs.

1. **Key Messaging Guide** (KMG): This reflects your brand voice, brand essence, brand story, and messaging hierarchy.

2. **Value Proposition** (VP): An articulated understanding of why parents 'buy' your school rather than another. It is usually one or two sentences.

3. **Strategy on a Page** (SoaP): A single page that expresses where you've been, your current reality, strategic priorities, focus of activities, and initiatives to execute. A single page is critical because it makes the strategy accessible and understandable to the whole school team, not just the marketers.

Once you've been through the DRIVE process, it's important to match your new strategy to actionable insights. Many strategic processes identify insights, but they can be confusing because they're not actionable or, if they are, the return for effort in executing them is minimal. Often, that's because marketing strategists help with the big picture, but lack the ability to draw the insights into a framework that gives guidance about how to execute it.

By contrast, at imageseven, it's insight applied. Once your school's strategy is agreed, we translate it into an action plan.

Insight applied

- Your school brand is not owned by you; it's owned by your stakeholders.
- Your brand is who you are, what you promise, and your ability and willingness to keep that promise.
- Bold School Brands always start with strategy first.
- Your communication and marketing strategy should be succinct, accessible, and actionable.
- Creating your Bold School Brand is too important to be left solely to marketers.

CHAPTER TWO

Business goals and objectives: Pick a direction and grow

Asking the tough questions to determine where to take your school and why.

On the dark and crowded forest floor, the young sapling has one goal — to grow towards the daylight. If it grows in the wrong direction or fails to reach the daylight, its competition will grow faster and quickly block out the sun, greatly reducing its chances of survival.

Brand strategy isn't so different. It begins with asking tough questions, setting goals, and choosing where to go. Competition can be fierce, but worse yet is not knowing in which direction to grow. Brand strategy is all about making future growth decisions. Before you decide which Pantone shade of orange your logo is going to be, or which keyword terms you want to dominate in Google searches, you need to make some intentional business decisions.

In the book *ReWork: Change the Way you Work Forever*, co-authors Jason Fried and David Heinemeier Hansson say that "planning is guessing." They're absolutely right. Goals you set today may be far too short-sighted and may even be laughable in 18 months' time. We're certainly not advocating a 200-page financial projection to begin your branding process, but it's hard to arrive somewhere if you never decide where you want to go.

At imageseven, we advocate a prescriptive brand strategy process when working with schools. It always begins with asking questions such as:

- What are your goals and objectives?
- Can you define your market, audience, and competition?
- How much money, time, and effort are you and your educators willing to invest to achieve your goals and objectives, support real change, and make your school stand out?

Perhaps you haven't thought through these questions. That's okay, but now is the time to wrap your head around them. By its nature, the branding process is very iterative. Future decisions are heavily influenced by the decisions you'll make today. Does that mean you can't change your mind in the future? Absolutely not. Continually adjusting objectives or tweaking your priorities are natural parts of marketing your school.

What are your goals and objectives?

That's a loaded question. Thinking about your school's goals is a big picture question. Big picture questions can be overwhelming to think through because sometimes they're so vague that it's difficult to consider them, or so general that any answer would be only partly correct.

Technically, this isn't one question. There are other questions behind it. So instead of viewing 'what are your goals and objectives?' as the question itself, think of it as the big bucket that carries lots of smaller buckets. Smaller buckets are the smaller questions and are easier to focus on. For many of our school clients, here's where we start.

- **What were your enrolments over the last three years?** What are your enrolment goals for this year, next year, and five years out? Are there any Years in which you would like to see more enrolments? Are there any Years that have become less profitable, that you'd like to de-emphasise?

- **What are your staffing goals for this year?** If you hit your enrolments goal, how will that impact your staffing needs? Is your senior leadership team missing any vital positions? Do you need more administrative help, more teachers, or more enrolment team support?

- **What are your student goals?** Do you need to retain more students? If you do, would that mean changing or expanding the subjects you offer, or offering more extra-curricular options? Or would you be better off servicing fewer students at a deeper, more profitable level?

- **What are your thought leadership goals?** Are you viewed as an expert in your field? Does the media come to you or to your competition for insights when something happens in the education sector? Do you have followers on social media?

- **Do you have a marketing goal?** Do you need to generate more leads for potential enrolments or to refine your current database?

- **Do you have a positioning or perception goal?** Do your current parents understand all that you do and the level at which you perform compared to your competition? Does the marketplace understand the unique value that you provide?

- **Where do your enrolment leads come from?** Are there particular lead generation tools that should be more productive for you, like open days, school expos, or your website?

- **What are your objectives for your website this year?** Do you want to improve your SEO? What keywords do you want to dominate? How many leads should your website generate? Do you need to improve your conversion rate (i.e. the percentage of parents who move from expressing interest to enrolling their child)? What are your social media goals?

- **What are you willing to invest to achieve your goals and objectives?** When you build a great brand, you invest more than money. You invest time, energy, and focus.

Cost

There's an old saying in the marketing profession that often gets used in other circles: "You can have it fast, good, or cheap. Pick two."

This applies to building a great brand. If this is what you want, you can do all the work yourself and spend more time on it, or you can get professional help and invest more money in the process to have it done faster.

What should a branding process cost? A conservative marketing budget should be somewhere between one and four percent of your annual revenue. If your school is new or faces stiff competition, you might consider upwards of ten to fifteen percent of gross revenue. A strong, differentiated brand is far more cost-effective to market than an unprofessional, me-too product or service. Branding costs can be viewed either as a capital investment or as part of your marketing budget. Regardless of where you decide to account for the expense, you need to consider your total marketing budget as a good place to begin.

Time

Who is going to be responsible for creating your new brand? Will you hire a branding firm or try to do it in-house? It's more than a question of budget; it's also a question of how much time you'll need to invest personally to see this come to fruition.

A branding firm should involve you with vital decisions during the process and keep you updated in more minor areas. Ideally, it should not be a total time-suck for you and your team. However, the more you carry on your own shoulders, the more you should expect to burn the midnight oil to get things right. You also need to consider the opportunity cost of doing it yourself. If you're working on branding, you're not doing your day-to-day work.

Another element of the time investment is your timeline. Is there an upcoming event for which you'd like to have your new brand ready? Is there a particular time of year that generates the most enrolments? We see many school clients who, once they've committed to a branding exercise, want everything done yesterday. Realistically though, developing a great brand takes time. Depending on the depth of the exercise and size of your school, expect to invest anywhere from several months to a year to properly position, rollout, and market your new brand.

Energy and focus

When a school is preparing to engage in a rebranding effort, one question that's usually asked is: "How much time are you going to need from me and my staff to make sure this is successful?"

There's no right or wrong answer here. Most education professionals like to feel as if they're leading anything they're hired to do. Everyone is used to being in control. Therefore, it's a good idea to discuss expectations from the outset. The bottom line is, it's important to understand the process and communication style of your branding partner. You'll want to have a good idea of how much input they'll need from you and your team, as well as how much ongoing legwork they'll expect from you.

Going back to our good, fast, or cheap example, if you selected cheap, there's a good chance you're going to have more work to do on your side of the fence.

Defining your market, audience, and competition

Once you've made it through the big questions of goals, objectives, timeline, and budget, these next few questions will seem like a cinch.

What is your market category?

Your market category should be a simple statement that identifies your brand's general sphere of competition.

For our school clients, we want to make sure their market category is crystal clear and as tightly defined as possible. It's natural to think that we're pigeonholing them by doing this, but if we don't get explicit, it will cause problems differentiating them later in the process.

For instance, instead of saying your school is targeting 'K–12 school students', we might say it's a 'K–12 school in the Anglican tradition serving families in Sydney's north-west', which will provide a clear marketing focus.

Of course, you know what your school does, but when you describe it to others, do they really get it? Once you put it on paper, your market category may surprise you. Or it may confirm what you already suspected was true.

Who is your audience?

Who are you targeting? Who do you want to know about your school? Where are they? Do you service a specific geographic area, region, or country? Is your focus domestic or international students? What do your parent profiles look like?

Again, we try to be specific with the answers to these questions, but there is often more than one audience type. For a 'K–12 school in the Anglican tradition serving families in Sydney's north-west', the main audiences may look something like this:

- Anglican parents living in Sydney's north-western suburbs whose children are already in a local kindergarten, primary school, or high school and who wish to move them to another school.
- Anglican parents living in Sydney's north-western suburbs whose children will soon enter kindergarten, primary school, or high school.
- Anglican parents about to move to Sydney's north-western suburbs who are looking for a kindergarten, primary school, or high school for their children.

Secondary audiences would be:

- Parents living outside Sydney's north-western suburbs who want their children to attend an Anglican school.
- Parents living overseas who want their children to attend an Australian school.
- Parents living in, or are about to move to, Sydney's north-western suburbs who want their children to attend an Anglican school but are not Anglican themselves.

Who is your competition?

If you're lucky, this is a short list. But most schools have competitors at various levels.

An independent Anglican K–12 school has to compete at some level, not just with other Anglican K–12 schools, but with local government schools, schools that aren't Anglican, and standalone kindergartens, primary schools, and high schools. For older students, there are alternatives offered by TAFEs and other registered training providers.

Sometimes it's less like comparing apples to apples and more like an apple, an orange and a banana.

As you list your competitors, think about them along the lines of the type of school (kindergarten, primary, etc.), price, quality, reputation, location, and religious affiliation (if any). List all your competitors in each category. From these lists, create a visual to show where your real competition is and where your positioning opportunities lie. This is called perceptual mapping. Specifically, this is your perception of your competition.

Then select two categories that make the most sense to compare. For example, you might compare quality versus price.

Create a simple chart with horizontal and vertical axes. Along the horizontal axis, map the elements of your competition's quality. At the left will be lower-end competitors and to the right will live more customised competitors. Now along the vertical axis compare pricing — the cheapest offerings live at the bottom and the higher you go along the vertical axis, the more expensive the offerings. Place marks not only where your school sits, but also where your direct and indirect competitors land.

After you plot this first chart, get creative. Compare other things like the school's facilities or ability to offer alternative pathways.

If your chart looks like Figure A over the page (low and to the left with lots of surrounding dots), you're probably a run-of-the-mill standard school. Your positioning opportunities are (a) command a higher price through value, brand, or service or (b) win more market share.

If you're in this space, focus on finding an intangible way to differentiate your product or service. In the 1940s, advertising legend Rosser Reeves called this 'thing' your Unique Selling Proposition (USP). Cola is just cola, right? Not if it's "the real thing."

If your chart looks like Figure B (high and to the right, with a few surrounding dots), you're likely a premium school. In the premium world, your positioning is already pretty set. You are distinguished and, as such, you charge more.

Where does your school fall on the map?

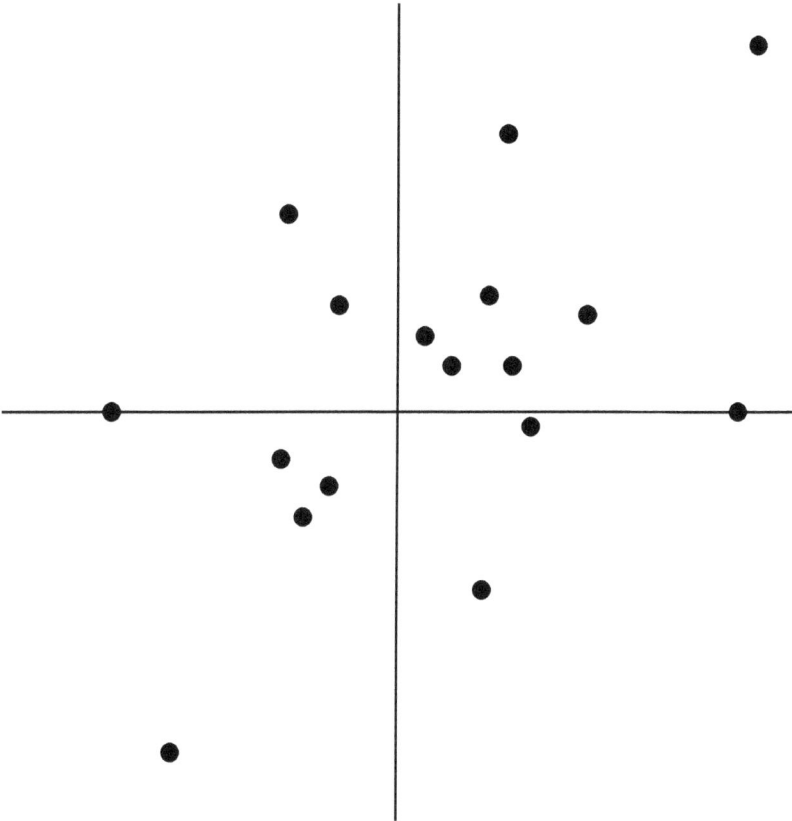

Figure A: **Standard**

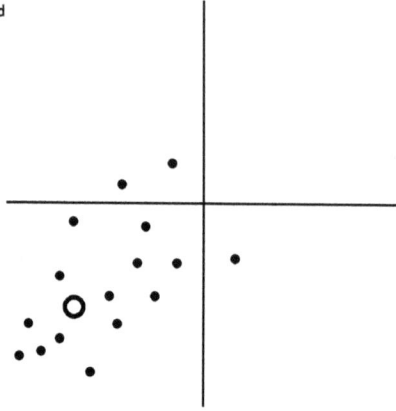

Figure B: **Premium**

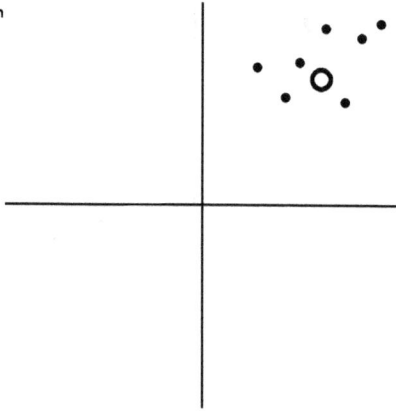

Figure C: **Crowded**

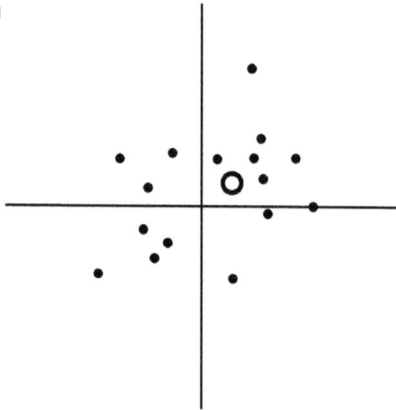

Positioning is less of a tool to explore and more of a status to maintain. Strong, consistent branding is the best way to maintain your premium status.

Conversely, if your chart looks like most schools (Figure C), you have several positioning opportunities. The middle of your chart is a crowded place, but the corners are opportunities. What offerings could you remove from your school to make it cheaper and dominate the marketplace? What could you add to charge three times more? Or how could you operate in the midst of the competition and still stand out? Perhaps you could leverage your USP or differentiate yourself through reputation.

Case study: Aligning brand promise with delivery

Our client was a regional, co-educational, K–12 day and boarding school.

They asked imageseven to review their marketing practices and help the school to create a sustainable marketing strategy.

During the discovery phase, we uncovered a significant disconnect between what they were marketing and what they delivered, particularly in relation to fees.

Before we helped them to create a strategy, the school revisited their enrolment practices and fee schedule. This created a solid foundation for considering their financial, enrolment, and marketing goals.

Their new marketing strategy reflected the reality of their current position, with an achievable pathway to their preferred future.

Within three years, the school reported their initial goals had been achieved for enrolment and finances.

Insight applied

- Marketing goals and objectives should be closely tied to your school's overall strategic intent.
- If your marketing strategy reveals incompatibility with your goals (or no goals), consider pausing it until you review your goals and can base the strategy on your revised strategic intent.

CHAPTER THREE

Positioning and differentiation

One of the biggest challenges for any school is figuring out how to be different. How do you stand out as a unique offering in the marketplace?

How do you look different and sound different from your competition? It's so tempting to jump straight into a purely visual exercise. But first you have to answer the question: "Who are we?"

What does your school stand for? What do you believe? Who are you, really? Are you different enough to be memorable? Positioning is the art and science of getting to the bottom of some of these questions.

Do you have a positioning problem? Many schools don't think so, at least not at first.

Have you ever had a parent share with you that they didn't know your school did something that you thought everyone know about? Can all your staff quickly rattle off an elevator pitch for your school and what you do — something that won't make you cringe? Does your receptionist know what your school specialises in? If your dream parent walked into your school while you were on vacation, would your team know what to do with that person — or even recognise him or her as a great prospect?

If any of these questions concern you, there's a good chance you have a positioning problem. Don't worry — most schools have a positioning problem at some level. They evolve, the market's needs change, new legislation makes an impact, and educational trends are continually in flux. Positioning is constantly in need of attention, but that's not an excuse to ignore it.

I'm thinking of a frog

Mr Waldron had a way of delivering new concepts unlike any teacher I've ever known. He sat motionless in his chair in the back corner of the room. My classmates and I were familiar with his behaviour, but today was somehow different. The lights were down low. Nobody knew if they were supposed to respond or just continue to sit quietly.

He started again: "I'm thinking of a frog."

"Kermit?" someone mused.

"I'm sorry, but that's not the frog I was thinking of."

"The little ones with the big red eyes? Is that the frog?"

"I'm sorry, but that's not the frog I was thinking of."

"It's when I can't seem to speak right? There's a frog in my throat?"

Again, he only offered: "I'm sorry, but that's not the frog I was thinking of."

Crap. What was it going to take for someone to figure this out?

Waldron taunted us again. "I'm thinking of a frog."

One of the students, a violinist, offered: "It's on my violin bow. It's the piece at the end that I hold."

"Yes, that is a frog," Waldron said with a little more pep. "But that's not the frog I was thinking of."

If you can imagine, this went on for the entire 90-minute period. And at the end of the class he simply said: "Have a nice day." No explanation. No debriefing. Just "have a nice day."

That single class messed me up. I think it left a lasting impression on all of us.

During our next class with Waldron, he explained that he wasn't thinking of any frog in particular. The point was to demonstrate how clearly we need to communicate. Even with such a specific noun as 'frog', the recipient of your message can be left very unsure of what you are trying to say. As I would later learn in a college communications class, 'message sent' does not equal 'message received.'

Today, I can't help but think of the parallels. Clarity and messaging. Positioning and marketing. Top of mind awareness and this thing we call brand.

People are thinking about 'frogs' — products, services, or solutions to their needs, wants, or incredibly difficult problems — all the time. They know exactly which frog they're thinking of, and there are several reasons why.

Will your school brand be the frog they think of first?

Josh Miles

There are many different elements to positioning.

Where are you located? How close are you to your potential students? Do they have to travel far?

Who is your ideal student? Do you target specific demographic or psychographic profiles? Do you target certain cultures, faiths, or age groups?

What do you do? Is your school unique or the same as your competitors? Are all your teachers highly experienced and well-qualified? Do you offer courses that other schools don't? Are your school's facilities outstanding? Do you offer students the latest technologies? What you 'do' is the tip of the positioning iceberg. When you're in the education sector, others can see this tip. However, there are many more things you do that are all but invisible to most existing and prospective parents.

Have you ever considered your mission or vision?

What are they? You need a real mission statement, not a motivational poster statement. This question can be a trap. We hate most mission statements with a passion, not because they're inherently a bad idea but because 99 percent of them are generic, bland, and forgettable.

At imageseven, when we think a client might not be grasping how much they look like their competition (or if their mission is articulated in the same way as everyone else's) we sometimes run an exercise with their leadership and marketing teams.

We visit three or four of their competitors' websites and copy their articulation of their mission. We then change the school names to our client's. In the next session, we announce that we've done some rough drafts of how we would like to articulate our client school's mission and brand story, but we want to get feedback on which version resonates with them. The discussion that follows is usually punctuated with statements like, "you've got it … that's us!" and "I agree that we're the leading school in our area." We then reveal that these are their competitors' articulations and suggest that if they want to stand out, they need their mission statement to capture their school's uniqueness.

It's not that most school mission statements don't sound nice. It's that they are trite, undifferentiated, and uninspired. Which school doesn't want to provide every student with the best possible education? Who doesn't want to produce a confident and exceptional student?

We give our school clients two choices here: Lose the mission statement altogether, or do it right.

The bottom line is that a weak mission statement often reflects poor positioning. Which should come first, the mission or the positioning? It can seem like a bit of a chicken and egg question. But we always prefer to begin by developing strong positioning then let the mission statement flow from that language.

We'll dive deeper into positioning in the next chapter.

But right now, let's talk some more about mission statements. If you're going to have one, it should be the guiding light that directs the course of your school.

Here are four approaches to writing a mission statement that people will understand.

First, focus on the facts.

What do you do? What's your educational offering? What's your market? How far is your reach? What words does your school use to describe what it does? This step should be pretty straightforward.

Second, think about the emotions.

How does your school make the world a better place? Who does it benefit? Who would miss it if your school disappeared? Why should anyone care? Make a list of some of the most emotionally charged benefits of your school. Still scratching your head? If you're stuck on this one, consider enlisting help from someone who knows your school well but has a more objective point of view. Once you've given this ample consideration, move on to step three.

Third, focus on the unique.

What's the one thing that your school does better than anyone else? Are you the best at it in your market or region? Can you claim uniqueness?

Complete this sentence: 'We are the only school in (blank) that does (blank).' When you fill in the blanks what do you get? If it sounds the same as your competition, you may need to dig deeper. Give this plenty of thought before moving on to the final step.

Finally, simplify, simplify, simplify.

Taking what may be several pages of notes from the exercises above, begin simplifying the message into statements. If you're really focused, you may be able to distil it down to a few succinct words.

A two-word mission statement isn't right for everyone, but if your mission is unclear, ambiguous or wordy, keep working.

A few more words of advice: The senior leaders of your school need to own the mission statement. Hiring a professional writer may be a good move, but you should limit who gets a vote on the final mission statement to avoid decisions made by committees.

That's important. No mission statement committees!

Are you communicating your positioning with the megaphone or the wedge?

Most school staff are so excited about their school's capabilities that they will bowl over their friends and family when trying to explain them. "We offer our students this, and this, and that, and even this other thing, but our specialty is [insert specialty]. Except last week, this one family asked us to do this totally different thing, so we thought we could probably figure it out. And then they asked us to help their child to do yet another thing. We didn't know anything about that stuff, but we eventually worked out how to do it! Do your kids need any of that?"

Imagine if you were the poor soul cornered by this person at a cocktail party or networking event. Even if you were trying to pay attention to the story, you'd likely walk away thinking the school was a Jack of all trades and master of none. The chances you'd remember it for its specialty are about nil.

The problem is, you were hit with the broadside of the school's capability iceberg. It's deep, blunt, cold, and too much for anyone to take. Even the Titanic couldn't handle the impact of the broadside of an iceberg.

Blair Enns, founder of the *Win Without Pitching* training program, is a business consultant to marketing and creative firms. He calls this sales tactic 'the wedge'. If you lead with the blunt side of the wedge, there's impact for sure, but it's too broad an angle to ever pierce your audience's armour. To do it right, you have to turn the wedge around and attack with the pointy part — the armour-piercing side of the wedge.

Let's go back to our cocktail party example above. Instead of listening to your friend, let's say you're the one who is asked: "So what does your school do?" Being a fantastic networker, you respond with something like: "We're a K–12 school in the Anglican tradition serving families in Sydney's north-west." One of several things is likely to happen next.

1. **Immediate need:** Your friend might immediately think of how this could help him or someone he knows. With one little tease, you have opened the door for him to learn more about your school. His earnest interest in learning more may sound like: "My wife and I are about to move to that area and we're having trouble finding a good Anglican school for our two kids. How can your school help us?"

2. **Plant the seed:** Although he may not have an immediate need, don't lose heart. Your words probably resonated with him on some level. "My kid says she's happy at her present school but who knows with teenagers. I'll keep your school in mind if that changes."

3. **A future lead:** Maybe your friend will be able to quickly determine your school is not a fit for his child. And that's okay. Sometimes there's a zero percent chance your new friend will ever be interested in your school but regardless, your pointy message will stay with him. The next time he is asked for a school referral, he might remember this conversation. His response will sound more like: "My kids are about to leave school but some of my friends are just starting to look for a high school for theirs. Give me your business card in case they ask me for school recommendations."

Regardless of how real the opportunity is once you've pierced the armour, the point is that you've pierced it. You've positioned your school for something very specific and are much more likely to be remembered by your new friend. Good work.

But how do you get to that armour-piercing positioning statement?

The trick is to get to a narrower positioning than many schools are comfortable with. Or, as we say in the marketing world, your goal should be to find your niche.

Chances are you aren't operating from a niche position today. You probably want to appear to offer everything to every student, because you think that will attract the maximum number of parents.

But let's think about that. Does your school have any competition?

Reading that question, you probably immediately thought of one or two competitors. Your prospective parents may even have asked you about them. After all, your competitors are busy pitching for the same parents that you're pursuing.

What if you could make those competitors go away? Not out of business, but unable to ever compete with your school? The reality is that you can't get them to go anywhere, but there is a very simple alternative.

Make your competition invisible by getting out of their business. Niche yourself so far away that you'll never see them again.

It's all about positioning. If you're familiar with the concept put forward by W Chan Kim and Renée Mauborgne in their international bestseller, *Blue Ocean Strategy*, finding an untapped, wide open market is awesome. The truth is, you may not have to be quite that radical. If you take a page out of Seth Godin's *Purple Cow* playbook and just do something remarkable, you're halfway there.

A great first step is to define a niche. "But I don't want to pigeonhole our school with a niche!" Yep, think of all of those poor, under-performing niche brands: North Face (just for hikers), Apple computers (just for creative types), and Nike (just for serious athletes).

Niche positioning doesn't limit your market — it expands it.

Why is that? Because when a consumer thinks, "I really need an XYZ," whatever brand fulfils that niche positioning will be the first brand they think of.

So how do we apply what we see in the consumer product market to the education market?

First, let's remember that the same thirty year old dude who's buying North Face and Apple could be the same professional who's making the decision about which school to choose for his seven year old. People are people. When they're at work, they're still people. You aren't selling to a business. You're selling to another person. Don't forget that.

Five easy methods to identify your niche

So, back to the question of how we can go about applying what we know in the consumer market to the schools market. Here are our top five suggestions.

1. Find a price niche.

What would your parents be willing to pay a premium for? What can you offer at the top end of the price spectrum? Or how can you bill differently? How would that impact your enrolment numbers?

2. Look for low-hanging fruit.

What do parents want that you (and your competitors) don't currently offer? How can you take your service to the next level? Daily videos of their child playing happily in your Kindergarten? Personal tutoring options in Year 11? Free lunchtime yoga or meditation classes for Year 11 students? Three months in Tokyo to polish up their Japanese language skills?

3. Before you try to look different, figure out how to be different.

Design and marketing professionals are experts in the art of creating something new and interesting. This works great when you are new and interesting. However, if you're really more of the same old, same old, it tends to backfire. Arguably one of the best 'brands' in history for doing something different was Barack Obama. He sounded different, he exploited his differences and he did an amazing job of looking different.

4. If you're doing something different, be sure to look and sound different.

Imagine this: You've designed a game-changing school offering. And now it's time to take it to market, you decide to mimic your closest competitor's brand identity, design, brand voice, and advertisements. Given all the similarities, why would anyone expect your service to be different to your competitor's, let alone better? If your aim is to truly be remarkable, take it all the way. Imitation in the world of branding is the sincerest form of shooting yourself in the foot.

5. Ask a trusted advisor.

Chances are, you're so close to your own brand that you're still a bit confused. You may have even convinced yourself that you're well-niched and highly differentiated. Strangely enough, your competition is still there, buzzing in your ear. Now would be a good time to get a second opinion. Ask a mentor, a colleague in a different profession, or an outside marketing professional for their thoughts.

Finally, here's a tip: If you decide to look for an outside firm to help with your positioning, branding, or marketing, ask them why they're unique. Then ask them who their competition is and do some research. If the first firm's answers about their competitive difference sound similar to their competition's, keep looking.

Case study: When perception is different to reality

Our client was an outer metropolitan, Christian, co-educational, K–12 day school that was low-fee and had been operating for 20 years.

They asked us to create a new brand to position the school as an established operator with a good track record and to prompt prospective parents to consider them.

The school had been started on a very tight budget. The visual identity needed to reflect reality as well as give staff an opportunity to believe the school was now well-established and presented a broader opportunity.

A series of discovery sessions revealed that the brand of the school — the perception of who the school was, what they promised, and their ability and willingness to keep that promise — differed significantly from the reality. The community and many of the staff still believed it was in startup mode and didn't have the resources to match the competition.

The visual cues reinforced this perception. The visual identity was complex, looked cheap, and had become significantly distorted and degraded through poor reproduction.

The original logo had tried to emulate a school of deep heritage and longevity to position it as an alternative to the high-fee, single sex competition. Unfortunately, this had a negative effect once the school became established enough to attract interest from beyond local church communities. The crest was trying to look old and prestigious, but the reality (the grounds and classrooms, low-fee pricing and poor-quality branding) was at odds with the brand positioning.

The truth was that the school was very well set up with technology. It was much more forward-looking than backward-looking. It had no historical hurdles to restrain its positioning.

A decision was made to develop a visual identity that was very clean and minimalist, clearly conveyed the Christian faith of the school, and positioned it as future-focused.

Fourteen years later, the school has grown in numbers and become the benchmark low-fee school in its locality.

Insight applied

- What you think you are saying could be very different to what your audience is hearing or understanding.
- An accurate understanding of your ideal family is vital.
- *Be* different before trying to *look* different.
- Your brand exists at the intersection of your promises and how your community experiences you.

Brand voice

> The voice of your brand isn't about who does your voiceover. It's about developing a common tone to the words and style of messaging that is unmistakably from your school.
>
> Crafting your brand voice is about writing from a position that plants the proverbial flag in your competitive landscape. The intersection of what you promise and what your parents and students experience is the very essence, the heart and soul of your brand.
>
> In this section, we will review a tool to keep your team aligned, three approaches to rebranding, and how to develop your school's brand voice.

What is your brand essence?

CHAPTER FOUR

The positioning brief: Finding your brand essence

How to keep everyone in your school on the same page.

Your Bold School Brand positioning brief

Branding and positioning exercises can be great team-building experiences for your senior leadership. It's exciting to embark on a rebranding process and it can be energising for everyone involved. But it will all be a waste of time if you don't make everyone within the school community aware of your new direction, from parents, students, and teachers through to governors and moral owners, such as churches.

To keep everyone on the same page, you need some type of document that will serve as a guide. When we work with a client on a branding initiative, we create a document that we call the Bold School Brand positioning brief. In this chapter, we walk through how you can follow the same process with your brand.

The Bold School Brand positioning brief is an internal document that ensures everything your school says, does, or plans — from branding, advertising, and orientation tours to lapel pins — consistently leverages the factors that set you apart.

Your Bold School Brand positioning brief should be organised into the following short sections:

- Your market category
- Who you are
- Who you aren't
- What you believe
- Your brand essence.

Let's look at each one.

Your market category

The goal here is to state your market category explicitly. This is a simple statement, usually four words or less. Don't elaborate on the school's development plan or delve into the Head's experience. Simply identify your school brand's general sphere of competition.

It's hard to make it clear how this works for schools without providing a lot of context, so here's an example using an architectural firm:

> We are architects of public spaces.

Your brand category probably won't surprise you very much; instead, it will probably confirm what you already suspected was true, in a very concise statement.

Who you are

This specifically addresses the factors that make your school unique. It references your school's physical, intellectual, or attitudinal aspects. In a single paragraph, it should touch upon the most striking attributes. For our architects, this might read:

> We design iconographic spaces that become the visual language of a community and the soundtrack of its life experience. We focus on sustainable approaches to new construction and historic preservation alike. Our buildings become the standard for how public spaces should feel.

Who you aren't

Pointing out who you are not can help your team get a clearer picture of exactly who you are. To that end, your positioning statement should provide information that helps you define your niche.

> We aren't strip mall designers or architects who find the cheapest way to create a project. We aren't disconnected from the community or merely involved in hopes of winning another award. And, most importantly, we won't use a material that will compromise aesthetics, integrity, or our planet when a superior option is available.

What you believe

At this point, we're less interested in mere description. This paragraph serves as a manifesto that helps the attitude of your school brand take shape. It reflects the values and emotional aspects of your brand. And that's important. Decisions are almost always based on emotion.

We believe our work is deeper than designing a building or a space. We believe we are designing the experiences of this generation and generations to come. We believe that your mood, attitude, and state of mind will be impacted just by being surrounded by our work. We believe iconographic architecture defines the very heart of a place.

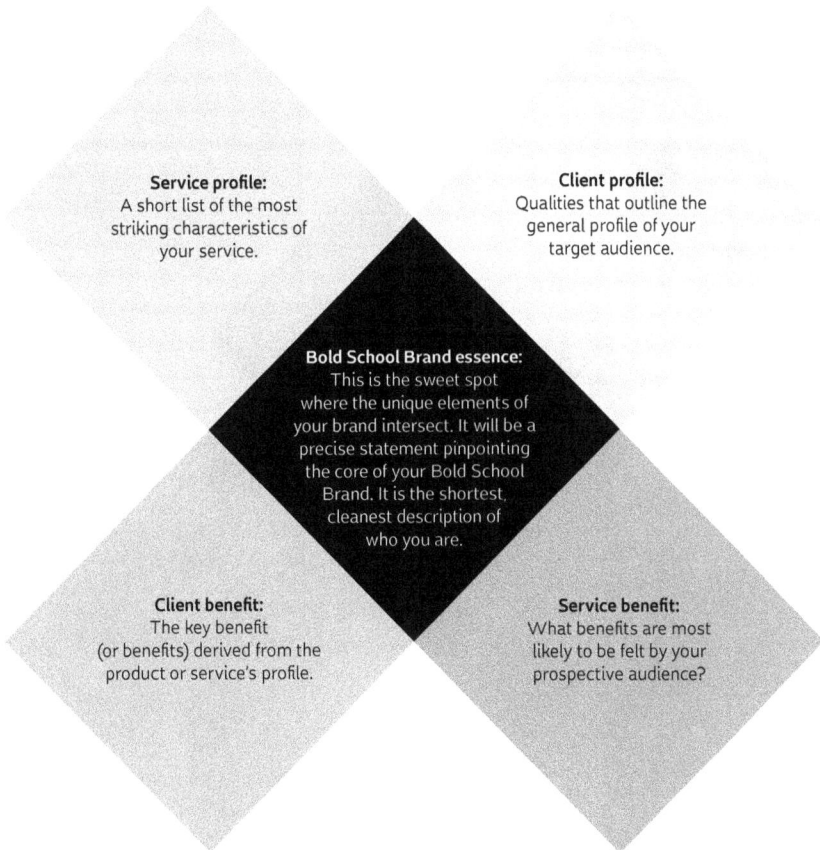

Service profile:
A short list of the most striking characteristics of your service.

Client profile:
Qualities that outline the general profile of your target audience.

Bold School Brand essence:
This is the sweet spot where the unique elements of your brand intersect. It will be a precise statement pinpointing the core of your Bold School Brand. It is the shortest, cleanest description of who you are.

Client benefit:
The key benefit (or benefits) derived from the product or service's profile.

Service benefit:
What benefits are most likely to be felt by your prospective audience?

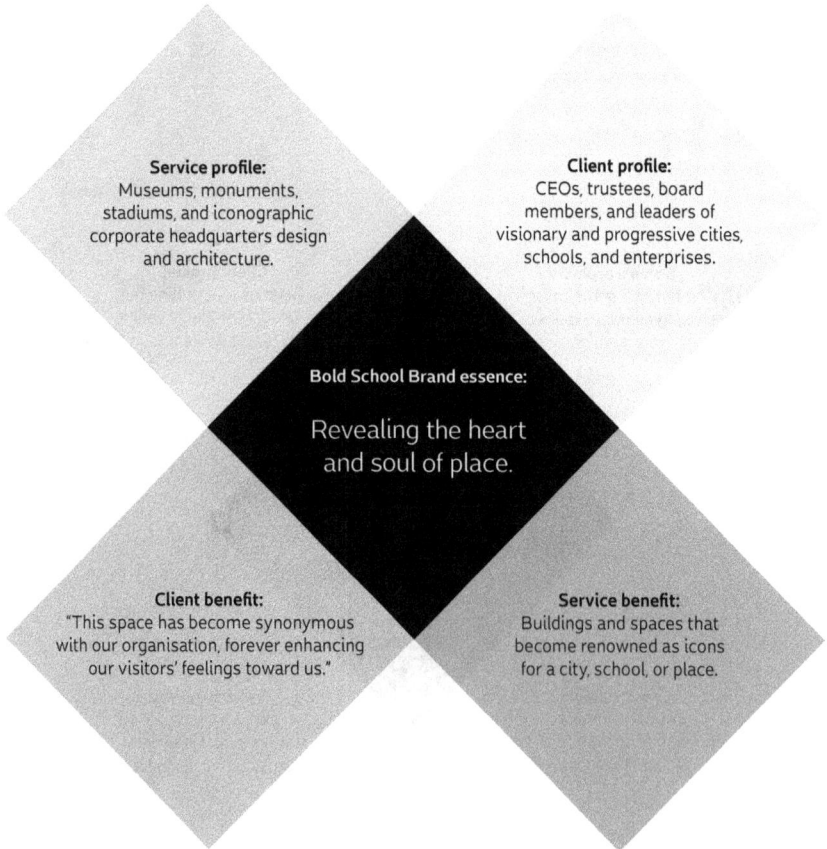

Service profile:
Museums, monuments, stadiums, and iconographic corporate headquarters design and architecture.

Client profile:
CEOs, trustees, board members, and leaders of visionary and progressive cities, schools, and enterprises.

Bold School Brand essence:

Revealing the heart and soul of place.

Client benefit:
"This space has become synonymous with our organisation, forever enhancing our visitors' feelings toward us."

Service benefit:
Buildings and spaces that become renowned as icons for a city, school, or place.

Your brand essence

What comes next? At this point, you have several stakes in the ground and a clearer idea about how your school intends to be viewed in the marketplace. You understand your competition, goals, values, and how you want to be seen. What you don't have yet is a single phrase from which you can articulate your position and your brand.

We believe this single idea — this single phrase — can be found at the point where the unique elements of your brand intersect.

How can you visualise this? Picture a giant X. The left leg is your school leg and the right leg is your audience leg. At the top of the X are your profiles and at the bottom are the benefits.

Again, we have used our architects as an example.

Offering profile

Create a short list of the most striking characteristics of your product or services:

Design and architecture for museums, monuments, educational institutions, stadiums and iconic corporate headquarters.

Audience profile

Think about the general profile of your target audience. Who are they and where are they found?

CEOs, trustees, board members, and leaders of visionary and progressive cities, schools, and enterprises.

Offering benefits

Explain the key benefit (or benefits) derived from your offering. Consider what really differentiates you.

Buildings and spaces that become renowned as icons for a city, school, or place.

Audience benefits

What benefits are most likely to be felt by your prospective audience? Any rules that we set in our previous chapter on mission statements apply here as well.

At the intersection of these four legs, you'll find your Bold School Brand sweet spot. From here, you'll be able to craft a precise statement that captures the core essence of your school's brand, i.e. your brand essence statement. It's the shortest, cleanest description of who you are.

When you see it all together, here's how the brand essence statement using our architectural firm example would read:

Revealing the heart and soul of place.

For many of our clients, the brand essence statement becomes an internal rallying cry, a tagline, or the building block for future voice and messaging exercises. A school's brand essence is unique, and people will have different opinions. For this reason, we often consider several alternative brand essence statements. It's like trying on a shoe — you'll know the one that fits best and feels most comfortable.

The brand essence chart is a powerful tool that helps schools visualise who they really are. In fact, one of our clients recently shared: "We've been trying to succinctly state who we are for years. We finally have something we can all point to and speak the same language. I love it!"

Case study: Distilling a brand essence from complexity

Our client wanted imageseven to capture the school's heritage and leadership position across all communication points.

It was a metropolitan, single sex, PreK–12, high-fee day and boarding school with well over a century of legacy and tradition.

The school was rich in stories and visual history, but its message was diffuse and scattered. This is the opposite to the problems most schools have when they consider their brand essence. This school had so much to draw on that its brand essence had become out of focus and inconsistent.

Finding the brand essence took three years and was carried out by the school leadership as part of their overall long-term strategic planning process.

The school's leaders looked back to the original intent and mission of the founders and looked forward to imagine how it would serve families in another 50 years.

The brand essence was distilled over time and ultimately expressed (from the marketing perspective) in a Key Messaging Guide. The brand essence was then used to influence every brand touchpoint: Website, imagery, copywriting, events, architecture, internal communications, staff professional development, online content, and, of course, marketing and advertising.

After just over a decade of consistent application of the brand positioning and brand management, the school is one of the most recognised schools across Australia and internationally.

Insight applied

- Understanding who you are and who you aspire to be is core to distilling and articulating your brand positioning.
- Taking cues from your heritage can be a useful starting point but you need to look beyond the 'what' to the 'why'.
- Your brand positioning implies that you stand for something. Many schools are not comfortable standing for something because they know that when they do, it means they don't stand for everything.
- Brand positioning for schools must be sustainable. Don't choose something that's flavour of the moment and that every school will do within a few years (e.g. robotics) or where your school relies on a particular staff member with expertise to drive it (e.g. an equestrian program).
- If committing to your brand positioning doesn't make you swallow hard, you may need to be even bolder.
- To effectively apply brand positioning requires much more than good communication and marketing practice. It requires consistent application to living the brand positioning at all levels.

Branding = problem solving.

CHAPTER FIVE

Three approaches to rebranding

There are three key reasons why schools rebrand and one of them isn't good.

In football, a team's approach is driven by one objective, which is to score more goals than the opposition. There are probably other things the team hopes to accomplish along the way. Improve its defensive strategy. Make fewer errors. But ultimately, it's about winning.

Likewise, as varied as the contributing factors may be for rebranding, a school's single goal can probably be boiled down to one thing: Make more impact.

There are a few different approaches that might help to achieve this goal, but before we dig into what these look like, let's first explore the contributing factors that lead to rebranding.

What drives a school to rebrand in the first place?

Schools choose to rebrand for a variety of reasons. Sometimes they rebrand to shed excess baggage or negative PR. Sometimes it's a merger with another school. Sometimes it's a shift in their approach or business model. And sometimes it's just time to dust off a dated look and refresh their position in the market.

When a school is willing to invest time and effort into rebranding, there's typically a problem to solve or a milestone to achieve. It may be an internal issue, such as poor morale, management, or lack of systems. It may be an external issue, such as an outdated appearance. It could be driven by a target to double enrolments or expand into a new market. Or it may be a combination of problems they seek to overcome and goals they hope to achieve.

Branding = problem-solving

At its root, isn't that what good branding does? It helps to solve problems.

The problem-solving characteristics of branding are derived from its roots in business strategy and design.

Wait a minute — design is problem-solving? Isn't design just another word for 'decorating'?

It's natural to think of design as the act of making something look better, prettier, cooler, or more cutting-edge. This very well could be what most people think the word means.

However, take a minute to look up 'design' in the dictionary. In most cases, you'll find a description of purpose, planning, intention, and thought behind something. It's important to see branding as an extension of this type of planning and intentional problem-solving. A branding exercise that doesn't seek to solve a problem will yield a lacklustre end product.

Branding isn't the only strategy that can help a school to achieve goals or solve problems. A variety of decisions could greatly impact its ability to reach new heights. It could choose to invest in infrastructure or staff, or relocate to a new, higher-profile location.

However, rebranding is an optimal strategy for any school to consider when seeking to solve an awareness problem. Those that choose to rebrand are likely to see their awareness problem as a primary roadblock to accomplishing their number one goal: Making an impact on the lives of students and their families.

Awareness takes many shapes

Any school that has been around for a while surely has some awareness in the marketplace. If not, they probably wouldn't still be there.

However, is it the right kind of awareness? What's the market's impression of the school? Does the target market understand the breadth of the school's capabilities?

Let's look at the different shapes that awareness problems may take.

No awareness

Awareness is a funny thing. A school may have an awareness problem because nobody knows they exist or they have simply been flying under the radar. Of course, their current parents and students are aware of them. However, if their goal is to reach more parents and grow enrolments, they need more awareness in the marketplace.

Consider when Australian fashion brand Cotton On broke into the US market. Americans thought this was a new brand, but it wasn't. Cotton On opened their first store in Victoria in 1991 and launched in the US in 2009. They enjoyed high brand awareness on their home turf, but now they needed to build it in their new market.

If people don't know about your brand, you have an awareness problem.

Unfavourable awareness

Another school may think the world has a negative impression of them. Whether this poor reputation is rightfully earned or not, it's an awareness problem that must be dealt with.

Limited awareness

Awareness also comes into play when your business model shifts or you add a new capability. Is the market aware of exactly what you do now, and why it should matter to them?

Brands that recently overcame this type of awareness challenge include the emergence of McDonald's in the gourmet coffee space. It was best known previously for its food offerings, and yet it has launched impressive campaigns for a space once dominated by Starbucks. Do you think of McCafé now when you want a cup of coffee?

Likewise, Hyundai has made an impressive push to be seen as a legitimate choice in the Australian SUV and 4WD market. Their fresh new product designs are evidence of an attempt to shift our awareness of their products and reposition their brands in the minds of Australian consumers. Is it working for you?

What other brands can you think of that have tackled their awareness problems? How did they solve these problems?

Solving awareness problems

Rebranding efforts most commonly fall under one of three approaches. We could explore others, but in the end, they could probably be classified as a variation of one of the following.

1. **Window-dressing:** "We have concerns with our reputation and our brand. Although many of our problems are directly related to our internal operations, school, and customer service, we hope our new look will help improve our reputation in the marketplace."

2. **A fresh face on a great place:** "We have a great school but a dated presence in the marketplace. We want our brand to be seen as positively on the outside as we see our school internally."

3. **Total brand overhaul, inside and out:** "Our brand is in rough shape. We have internal problems and problems with market perceptions. We know it's time to overhaul how we do things and we're thinking through every possible touchpoint, both inside our school and in the marketplace."

Let's look at each one.

First approach: Window-dressing

It's not uncommon for organisations in any sector that are dealing with internal problems to think that updating their look may help to improve public perception and, ultimately, their bottom line. However, if this window-dressing isn't accompanied by real change within, the rebranding effort at best will flop, and at worst will completely backfire.

So what's wrong with simply wanting your brand to look better?

Nothing — just be sure that the visual update is accompanied by real change in whatever is wrong with the school.

If you think a little window-dressing can solve your brand's reputation issues long-term, you're fooling yourself. Any time a school rebrands but fails to live up to its new image, that's an approach that isn't good.

Unfortunately, we've seen this with some of our past clients at imageseven.

Not many of them go into rebranding thinking "we'll just stop at a new look." When this does happen, it's usually a school that's failing to commit enough resources to

1

WINDOW-DRESSING
A FAKE FACADE
TO COVER UP A
POOR REPUTATION

2

A FRESH FACE
IMPROVING THE
IMAGE / AWARENESS
OF A STRONG SCHOOL

3

TOTAL OVERHAUL
COMMITTED TO
IMPROVING BOTH
INSIDE AND OUT

4

JUST BECAUSE?
REBRANDING YOUR
SCHOOL BECAUSE
YOU CAN

A brand that fails to live up to its promise is a LIE.

living its brand to the fullest. It's sad to see all the energy that goes into a rebrand wasted because of time, budget, or — worst of all — because the school never really intended to change and improve.

It doesn't matter how genius your strategy is, how beautiful your new visual identity may be, or how compelling your new stories, brochures, or website are. If your school can't stand behind the rebrand and live up to the promises it makes, your brand will quickly stand for something you didn't envision: Deception.

The reality is, a brand that fails to live up to its promise is a lie.

Sound harsh? It may be, but that's the truth.

You've probably seen this in play before many times.

"'Thank you for calling XYZ Mobile. Please enter your 14-digit account number followed by the hash. Your call is very important to us. Please continue to hold for the next available customer service representative."

The minutes tick by. You're drowning in easy listening hold music, interrupted every 15 seconds by the same "your call is very important to us" message.

After what seems like an eternity, a customer service representative mumbles, "Thank you for calling XYZ Mobile. My name is Roberta. Can you please verify your 14-digit account number?"

(Uh, okay.) "Sure, it's 3-4-2 ..."

"Thank you, can you please verify your mobile number?"

(Grrr.) "Uh, yes. It's ..."

"Thank you." (silence) "I'm sorry, our computers are really slow today." (Right, like it's just today.) "Okay, what can I do for you today?"

"I'm going to be in Bali next week. I just want to be sure my phone and email will work while I'm away. Can you help me with that?"

"I'm sorry sir, I'll need to transfer you to another part of customer service to assist with this need. May I transfer you now?"

(Sigh.) "Okay, thanks."

The phone rings through to another customer service representative.

"Thank you for calling XYZ Mobile. Please enter your 14-digit account number followed by the hash ..."

Regardless of what you thought of this brand or their service before this call, they've demonstrated very little interest in you as a customer during this interaction.

Second approach: A fresh face on a great place

Putting a fresh face on your school may sound like a similar approach to the window-dressing example. The crucial difference is that with this approach, the school is already known and well-respected by its current stakeholders.

So why would such a school want to update its image? Chances are that its visual identity has become dated and the appearance of its brand may be a detractor as prospective parents compare it to the competition.

In the end, schools pursuing this rebranding approach often want to better showcase themselves as fresh, relevant, and cutting-edge. A rebrand is a way to signal change to the marketplace — inviting people to reconsider the school because it has changed.

Most importantly, it has the chops to back up this claim.

If all your school needs to do is dust off its image, great things can happen quickly.

Consider the rebrand of American logistics company UPS in 2003. Their primary service had not changed in practice. They remained an international player in the shipping business. They were known for their approachable and courteous delivery drivers.

Unfortunately, their previous logo (designed in 1961 by design legend Paul Rand) was becoming, practically speaking, a bit dated. While the colours and typography were nearly timeless, the 'bow' in the logo represented a hand-tied string around a package. UPS hadn't allowed string around their packages for years.

What followed was a logo and overall brand update. The new identity was simple and looked 'fast' (more befitting of their racing sponsorships). In addition, their new slogan, "What can brown do for you?" quickly became part of the American public lexicon.

UPS was already a strong, well-respected company, but its brand refresh helped put a new face on a great place and lifted them to even greater success in the shipping business.

Third approach: Total brand overhaul, inside and out

Schools that completely overhaul their brands must be committed to change, both on the inside and in how they are perceived from the outside. When an overhaul is done well, every possible brand touchpoint is examined thoroughly, asking "how could we make this better?"

Rebranding at this level can be a long, expensive, and challenging undertaking, but when done well, is worth the investment and is a holistic approach we always favour.

This type of rebranding is also the easiest to spot. You can actually see a different school arise from the ashes of its previous self. Internally, you can spot happy teachers who rally around what the brand stands for. Externally, you can see the evidence of where the brand plans to grow.

This is the type of energy we saw in the late 1990s, when Steve Jobs returned to Apple, reinvigorating the leadership, product line, and public perception of the company he had co-founded.

Which approach will you take?

If you're considering a rebrand, it's essential that you focus on every touchpoint of the brand, not the least of which is how your school performs and delivers on what the brand promises.

The goal is not only to develop the workings for a great brand, but also to create a clear picture of how to live out that brand every day. With the guidance of a Bold School Brand positioning brief, a rebrand will lead to authentic improvements, both internally and externally. But much like a playbook, if you don't go back to the document regularly, it's easy to be tempted to cut corners and forsake much of the intended brand architecture.

Be intentional in how you proceed with a rebrand. Be true to your vision and avoid the window-dressing approach. Parents and teachers alike can sniff out a brand that's not being true to itself.

Case Study: Three approaches to rebranding

Client #1

This metropolitan, co-ed, K–12, low-fee day school wished to use branding to improve the school's perception in the marketplace.

It had experienced a bad run with leadership — several school Heads had only lasted a year. There were also problems with staff, brand consistency, internal organisation, and finances. The new Head felt the need to break the perception cycle of existing staff and parents.

He consciously gave his messaging a tilt towards goals and aspirations beyond his first year. Although good, this alone wasn't enough to quell distrust among staff and parents, so he sought a rebrand that would serve two purposes:

- Fix some practical visual identity issues, as multiple school Heads had not maintained brand consistency.
- Make the lift in the brand expression noticeable to stakeholders to let them know that the Head cared about the school community and its mission, and intended to be around for a long time.

This Head is still at the school and it continues to improve and grow, setting new enrolment records each year.

Client #2

A regional, single sex, PreK–12, high-fee day and boarding school sought to use branding to lift its image to reflect the reality that it truly was an outstanding school.

The school had a proud tradition, and was loved and appreciated by parents, students, and alumni alike, but the view from the outside was of a high-fee school that did things in a haphazard way and didn't have its act together.

A rebrand was undertaken that didn't change the brand assets but refined them and ensured they were used consistently. Along with a significant lift in the quality of collateral design and a website upgrade, the school was, over time, able to turn perceptions around.

It wasn't only about the brand. The school made a concerted effort to lift its good performance to new heights.

The school is now known as the benchmark for its market.

Client #3

Two existing schools were merging to create a single metropolitan, co-ed, Year 7–12, low-fee day school. We were asked to create an entirely new Bold School Brand.

We considered all the factors about the existing brands:

- The desire to not have one single brand be the 'survivor'.
- The desire to keep the best parts of both schools' cultures.
- The desire to create a new school with values articulated differently.
- The necessity to keep all stakeholders engaged and retain enrolments.

This is one of the rare cases where it was appropriate to execute a total brand overhaul in a school context.

Parents and staff were consulted throughout the process and kept abreast of developments. During the 18 months between the announcement and launch of the new school, significant time was spent on articulating the brand's key messages, selecting a new name, designing a new visual identity, consulting, and more consulting. The new brand was executed over the Christmas holidays, so students returned to a 'brand new' school.

The school now enjoys record enrolments.

Insight applied

- Schools, by nature of their status in the community, have built up more brand equity than most Heads appreciate. A total brand overhaul should therefore be given in-depth consideration, because it's a long road to completion.
- True rebrands are much more than a new logo or school crest. Consider who you are and what you promise, in order to decide what type of rebrand is required.
- At its core, a rebrand should solve a problem. Be clear about the problem you want to solve and how your intended course of action will take you closer to solving it.

CHAPTER SIX

An ownable voice

Often, a rebrand doesn't go much further than skin-deep. You need to create a brand voice that is as unique and ownable as your new look.

When most school Heads think of a rebrand, they probably picture a different look and feel, an updated logo, and hopefully a new positioning strategy. Maybe (if they're really thinking ahead) they'll consider a fresh tagline or even another name.

But often, a rebrand doesn't go much further than skin-deep. When the website and marketing materials get spruced up, how many schools redo the copy on the pages, the headlines, the voicemail messages, or the instructions on online forms? Very few.

Do you remember when you were in primary school? If your school was anything like ours, when the weather didn't cooperate during recess, we had to stay in our classrooms and play games. One of them was the telephone game.

Everyone sat in a big circle. The teacher would whisper a phrase in the first student's ear. Their job was to remember the phrase as closely as possible and repeat it to their neighbour. Of course, as the message went around the circle, it got more and more distorted. Sometimes, by the time it reached the end of the circle, the original phrase was completely changed. At best, the meaning of the underlying message was occasionally maintained, but often the intended meaning became jumbled and was unrecognisable as the original phrase.

Every now and then, a phrase would make it all the way through, unscathed. Why would some work well and others completely fail? There's a good chance it had a lot to do with the original message. Phrases that made it all the way around the circle were usually short, concise, and simple. Of course, it didn't hurt if the phrase was humorous or unexpected. Short and to-the-point phrases promised much better outcomes around the telephone game circle.

A school's messages are no different. Headlines, taglines, elevator speeches, and mission or vision statements are the building blocks of what we call a brand's voice.

Create a unique brand voice

Your brand's voice isn't a one-liner. Nor is it a programmed way of speaking. It is, however, very intentional. Many young brands make the mistake of coming off either too lock step in their voice, or their marketers have an innate fear that having a scripted baseline for communications will yield a fake-sounding brand. These are two extreme views, and neither makes for a very compelling experience.

One quirky brand with a distinct voice is the email marketing company Emma.

The marketing team at Emma has a clear idea of what they want their brand to look and sound like. The voice is casual and friendly, and there is almost always an undertone of humour in their messaging. Every communication from Emma lets the reader feel like he or she is sharing an inside joke.

Would this voice work for a very academic school? Probably not. But it does help a software company sound human and personal. Not an easy feat for a service that's sold almost entirely online and over the phone.

Stop for a moment to think about how a one-paragraph biography for an average software executive might sound. Now, take a look at the bio for one of Emma's founders:

> "Will Weaver is one of the co-founders here at Emma. He sets the design direction and coordinates all things technological. He is also very tall. It was Will who proposed one afternoon in late 2001, over assorted coffee drinks, that a company be started, one that might create a web-based service to help businesses of all shapes and sizes. Being the tallest person at the table, others felt inclined to listen and, during pauses in conversation, to nod vigorously. Before helping start Emma, Will served as the Web Director for Nashville-based custom-publisher Hammock Publishing and as a founding member of Smallbusiness.com. Will is a graduate of The University of The South, known in more casual circles as Sewanee."

As you may notice, this bio still drops in some important corporate details about Will, but it does so in a very non-traditional style. We can find his title, his role, schooling, and background. What's missing, however, is a fluffed-up paragraph of unimportant job descriptions.

What makes Emma's voice so great is that they know not only who they are, but also who they're talking to. Advertising and design firms are a large part of their potential client base, and they know what it takes to stand out to companies that specialise in helping other companies stand out. It has to be fresh, unexpected, and consistent.

Every year, Emma holds a call-for-entries for a non-profit they can donate their services to. Here's a snippet from their request for entries.

"Know a small, deserving non-profit in your neighbourhood? Think they could do even more incredible work with the help of a free Emma account? Are people giving you funny looks because you keep saying 'yes' to your computer?

"Well then, question-answering friend, it's that time of year to nominate a non-profit for the Emma 25. It's an annual Emma tradition where we team up with you to award free Emma service to 25 non-profits around the world, plus an additional 25 groups in cities Emma calls home — Nashville, Portland, Denver, and Austin."

Even when extending the brand to a social cause, Emma maintains its quirky voice. For more information about Emma, check out MyEmma.com, and be sure to read some of the deeper content for some real copywriting gems.

Cover up the logos

So, does a brand have to maintain a quirky or humorous tone to be memorable? Of course not. The off-beat language used by Emma is just one example. Your brand voice may be friendly, knowledgeable, technical or very serious. Is your language as differentiated as your positioning? Here's one way to tell.

Open your website next to your competitor's website. Cover up the logos and begin reading. If the copy sounds like either school could have said it, you've probably got some work to do.

Find a voice you can own

Practically speaking, how does a brand begin to develop its own voice? Start simple, with something we've already talked about — your Bold School Brand positioning brief.

Take a look at your audience section. Think of a few of your current parents in each audience category. What types of things do they like? What type of voice might they respond best to? Are you speaking to Millennials, Gen-Xers, or Baby Boomers?

In finding the right voice, don't feel like you can't use certain styles. Scientists may respond just as well to humour as ad agency executives, but the technique may require a different approach. The key is to find the style of voice that will best communicate with each target audience.

Also consider how you want your brand to be perceived. If you're interested in maintaining a sense of reverence and respect, overt humour or playful copy is probably the wrong direction to take your voice.

After considering audience and perception, think about how your competitors sound.

Some schools become parodies of themselves, especially when it comes to their brand voice. Picture how many car dealer ads blend together. Even their on-lot presentations of raised hoods, balloons, streamers, and neon window paint scream "what's it gonna take to get you in this car today?"

If every car dealership in town has a twangy, high-pitched, yell-at-the-screen male voice, perhaps a professional-sounding woman would stand out in the crowd.

Or maybe if your car dealer made you feel like they'd help you research and find the ideal vehicle for your family, wouldn't that feel different than having the latest sale screeched at you?

This type of approach is what we call an 'ownable voice'. It would be unique to the brand if no other car dealer was positioning itself as your expert guide. It's a voice that over time would be closely associated with that brand, and that brand alone.

An example from the education world is The Scots College, Sydney (NSW). When imageseven first started working with them in 2007, we reviewed their photography assets. Some were exceptional and most were very good, but the library had been developed without any visual direction or consistency. We found a photographer who understood the importance of visual brand consistency and storytelling. Now the College undertakes a photo shoot every year that updates and expands its image library. Images have become an integral part of the brand and many can identify a Scots image solely by its style and storytelling.

Put your voice into practice

After you've thought through your school's audience and style, write down all the things about your voice direction that you've decided on.

Let's go back to our car dealer example and call them Safari Motors.

Safari Motors has chosen a calm, expert voice — a cross between a surgeon and a zoologist. The voice is helpful, guiding, and professional. For verbal ads, they've decided to use female voice talent whenever possible.

The Safari Motors voice is:

> The professional and knowledgeable experts to help you find the perfect car for your family.

If you've done this well and have been honest with yourself, your voice statement and your brand essence should pair together like a gourmet dish and the perfect glass of wine.

Start making headlines

Armed with your voice statement, you might take a stab at writing headlines.

Be warned, this isn't as easy as you might hope. Most people who are not trained writers are just about as skilled at writing headlines as they are at writing mission statements. Many novices will fall into the trap of writing headlines that are strikingly similar to those of their competitors without even trying. This is a great spot to enlist the help of a professional copywriter. It's money well spent.

Here are a few ideas a professional copywriter might come up with for Safari Motors:

> "It's easy to spot a deal. Unfortunately, it's harder to find your perfect car."

> "We'll help you explore your options. Safari Motors."

> "Shouldn't finding the perfect car be just as easy as finding a good deal?"

Writing great copy isn't easy, but 'the first one has been done for you' approach may help if you're feeling uneasy about having a professional rewrite hundreds of pages of copy on your website. Contract them to write the most important and most highly trafficked pages. After that, you may feel more comfortable following along in a similar voice to flesh out the remaining elements or pages.

A few sample headlines probably aren't enough to get the hang of the voice, but a few essential website pages might be. It's all a matter of comfort level, and how quickly you can adapt to your copywriter's style.

Which message in your ad is *most* important?

(stock happy student photo goes here)

And will we ever find it? Yikes.

Lorem ipsum is often used as placeholder text in the body of an ad or layout. Typically the final text that is dropped in is either shorter or longer than intended. It's always best to start with the actual text, then layout second. Here's really where the "meat" of your mes-sage will probably go, so don't lose it in too much text.

Call to Action: Stop by any location for details

- Location Number One
- Location Number Two
- Location Number Three

Logo Goes Here

your tagline here.

1800 000 000   www.visitourreallylongweburl.edu.au

Disclaimer: Here are all the reasons that you won't ever actually be able to qualify for this offer, again probably way too much text. Sorry legal department — but is this really necessary?

Official Service of the Home Team.   Member: ▲●■

Does your ad suffer from acute tagline-itis?

Elevator pitch

Your elevator pitch is basically the intersection of your brand voice and your brand essence. It's often used in networking circles (as we illustrated previously) and should be brief enough to get across in no more than three sentences.

We often encourage clients to break their two- or three-sentence elevator pitch into a tease with a payoff. If your tease isn't enough to draw out a few questions, that person probably isn't much of a prospect to begin with. However, if your elevator pitch can be shortened into a memorable, compelling one-liner, that will do just fine.

Going back to our car dealer example, here are two different ways a Safari Motors salesperson might phrase their elevator pitch.

One-liner:

"... and what is it you do?"

"I'm a family fit specialist at Safari Motors. I help families to identify the best vehicle, then we help them to find the best deal."

Tease:

"... I'm a customer sales rep at the local bank; how about you?"

"I help families find their perfect vehicle using some techniques you'd expect, and one that you wouldn't."

"... uh, and what technique would that be?"

"Me! I only get paid if I help my clients find the best fit and the best deal for them."

See how that's a different approach and how it might yield a different response from a potential client?

Of course, the teaser line may be the perfect segue into a deeper discussion about your experience, teamwork, or approach. Longer conversations should be somewhat scripted as well (using a bullet point approach), but the conversation should maintain a natural flow and not feel staged or stiff.

Your tagline: Saying what's best for you

Unlike most other voice and copy elements we've discussed, the tagline is not something you absolutely must have. Certain brands are better suited to using taglines than others. Sometimes a school may have one, but often not.

Who has a great tagline?

Most people are familiar with some famous B2C or retail taglines: Nike's "Just do it." VB's "For a hard-earned thirst." L'Oreal's "Because you're worth it."

But what about school taglines? These are a little harder to come by, but here are a few examples:

"Brave Hearts Bold Minds." The Scots College, Sydney (NSW)

"Inspired by the Past, Embracing the Future." St Ignatius' College Riverview (NSW)

"Growing hearts and minds." Eltham College (VIC)

"More than an education." St Norbert College (WA)

"By daring & by doing." Wesley College (WA)

"Dare to be More." MLC School (NSW)

So does your school need a tagline?

This really comes down to your messaging strategy and how you would like your school's story to be told. The most awkward use of a tagline is when you can't really tell which line is the payoff to the copy, which is the tagline, and which is the school's motto.

In other words, some school brands get stuck in the rut of tagging everything — the headline, the body copy, the logo, and even the call to action.

The best recommendation we can make is to think through how you might want to use a tagline before you spend too much time writing it, let alone paying someone else to write it for you.

An unclear messaging or tagline strategy quickly becomes confusing — not just to your audience, but also to the team trying to assemble the communication pieces.

Make a tagline reduction

So, how do you create a tagline? Let's first assume you've thought through how you want the pacing of your messages to work, and you've decided a tagline would be a beneficial addition. Second, let's assume you have a strong Bold School Brand positioning brief, a powerful brand essence, and a compelling elevator pitch. If so, you're ready to create a tagline reduction.

In gourmet cooking, some of the most flavourful sauces are created through a process called reduction. It slowly cooks away the excess liquid by evaporating the mixture down to only the remaining ingredients. It yields a thicker and more flavourful sauce.

If you think of your Bold School Brand positioning brief, USP, and elevator pitch as your ingredients, your tagline goal should be to decide which 'flavours' of your brand you want to call attention to.

In the case of more descriptive brands (i.e. the name says what it is), such as Cheezels, your tagline goal may be more inspirational — for example their tagline, "Finger-licious fun." In the case of a less descriptive brand name, you may choose a tagline that describes or defines your USP. In short, the tagline should describe the most unique elements of your brand.

For many of our clients, if their brand essence is spot-on, it either becomes the platform for writing their tagline or becomes the tagline itself. Typically, the brand essence contains the right idea, but it's intended for an internal audience; so don't be frustrated if you need to rethink how to phrase it so it works as a tagline. Here again, you may want to enlist the services of a professional copywriter. A skilled writer can help you distil your USP into a marketable phrase for a memorable tagline.

In the case of our imaginary car dealer, a few possible taglines could include:

Safari Motors. Discover a new experience. (inspirational)

Safari Motors. Accelerate your search. (problem-solving)

Safari Motors. A lot of help. (silly pun)

Safari Motors. You've found your navigator. (emotional)

Safari Motors. Working with us is a trip. (fun)

MISSION

- Specifies who you are and what you do.

- Goes beyond commitment to quality.

- Is driven by your voice and positioning.

- Answers: "Why do we matter?"

VISION

- Is driven by your goals.

- Is aspirational.

- Is future-facing.

- Answers: "Where are we going?"

Can you think of some other tagline concepts for Safari Motors? What are a few descriptive options? How about another emotional direction? How would another inspirational tagline sound?

Mission statements

A good time to write a mission statement is after you've really dug into your brand voice. It's not that you wouldn't be able to talk about what your school does and why it matters without your newfound voice. The problem is, if you try to write your mission before you carve out your brand voice, your mission may not sound like your brand.

If you've ever written a mission statement before you developed a brand voice, you'll understand. So at the very least, treat that pre-voice mission statement as the scaffolding and build the right mission statement around it, then complete with your brand voice to give it that unique flavour.

Who needs a vision statement?

If you have all the other tools, why would you choose to have a separate vision statement? Let's explore a few possible reasons.

A mission statement focuses on who you are, what you do, and why it should matter. A vision statement is more of a future-facing, or even aspirational, statement.

Mission
- Specifies who you are and what you do.
- Goes beyond commitment to quality.
- Is driven by your voice and positioning.
- Answers the question, "Why do we matter?"

Vision
- Is driven by your goals.
- Is aspirational.
- Is future-facing.
- Answers the question, "Where are we going?"

The mission statement for our car dealer could sound something like this:

> "At Safari Motors, our mission is to be a guiding lighthouse to our clients in a sea of sales-focused sharks. We help families to find the best deals on only the vehicles that are the best fit for their lifestyle using the best technologies and tools, and we're willing to stake our reputation on our high-tech, high-touch promises. If we can't deliver, we don't expect them to buy from us."

It's a pretty compelling statement about how Safari Motors plans to do business on a daily basis, but it leaves out a few details about where they hope that approach will take them. The vision statement expands on those details:

> "Our vision is for Safari Motors to be the most highly rated car dealership in Victoria. Because our approach is different than just pushing deals out the door, we will probably never sell the most cars, and that's okay. Only by sticking to our values and demonstrating the benefit of our one-of-a-kind approach to client education and guidance will we become one of the top ten dealerships in Victoria in overall sales."

How will you set your vision? Going back to your Bold School Brand positioning brief, what were your overall goals? What's driving you to get there? What does the future look like for your school brand? With your mission as direction, where are you aiming to hit?

Go and find your voice

As you can see, there are many elements that go into developing a great, ownable voice for your brand. Frankly, it's an exercise that many schools don't take the time to do well. Given that fact, developing a brand voice is a terrific opportunity for you to further differentiate your school.

Case study: Creating a school voice

This was a long-term project with an ongoing client: A metropolitan, co-ed, K–12, mid-fee day school wishing to create a consistent voice.

Over three years, through key communications, we crafted a voice for the school that was close to the Head's natural voice, but slightly more authoritative than they would normally use to communicate. This became the voice of the school.

Official communications to the school community were factual and friendly, but with an authoritative stance — everything was backed up by fact. There was no "I believe" and lots of "research has shown us ... so we do this." Internal communications were, where appropriate, occasionally sprinkled with a little self-deprecating humour, because the voice of the school was saying, "we're at the top of our game, we want to stay there, but we don't take ourselves too seriously."

We consciously kept the occasional humour out of public documents and the website because it created a nice contrast when prospective parents came to the school and met the Head. They were able to see a little more of the school leader and have a sense that they had peeled back a layer and seen inside the school they were considering.

Over time, we noticed that senior staff adopted elements of the voice and incorporated it into their own communications.

Insight applied

- For most schools, an ownable voice occurs in a relatively narrow corridor between formal academic and friendly pastoral.
- It's important not to stray too far from reality when creating an ownable voice for your school, as you risk being inauthentic and damaging your brand.
- A school is more than its Head. As well as the school leadership, there are many staff with whom parents interact personally, so they have intimate knowledge of the usual or natural 'voice' of each person. This should also be taken into account when creating a school voice.

Brand identity

> Creating a great trade mark is only one element in developing a compelling brand identity system, and your brand is more than just a logo. A brand identity system is just that: A visual system to guide the development of brand collateral and marketing assets.
>
> It's a holistic combination of elements working together to motivate, inspire, and create change.
>
> In this section, we'll discuss what makes a great trade mark and how to build your brand collateral.

Disclaimer: This book is not intended by any means to be used as legal advice, but we want to provide a general overview of the many elements you need to consider and be aware of when developing a logo or trade mark for your brand. Always consult with a registered and reputable trade mark attorney before proceeding with any trade marking process.

CHAPTER SEVEN

Brand identity 101: How to develop, use, and protect great trade marks

Developing a powerful visual identity system is more complex than just designing a cool school crest.

By now, you've established what you intend your school brand to be known for in the marketplace. You've got a rock-solid Bold School Brand positioning brief that outlines your goals and objectives. You understand what makes your brand different. You have a memorable elevator speech. And you've developed a unique, ownable brand voice.

If you've been nodding to all these statements, you've built a solid foundation for what's coming next. We're finally at the stage where the branding exercise begins to express itself visually. Now is the time to begin building (or recreating) your brand's visual identity.

Like much of what we've covered so far, when it comes to creating your visual identity, engaging a well-respected branding or design firm will be a wise investment. As we continue, we'll find out just how complex this step in the process can be.

My neighbour is an artist ...

Just because your spouse, nephew or neighbour has a flair for the artistic, it doesn't mean they are going to understand how to develop a great logo or visual identity system. As the cornerstone of all your future marketing efforts, you owe it to your school, your staff, and your parents to do this well. Unless, of course, your spouse, nephew, or neighbour is an experienced branding or design professional. But even then, be sure they are being fairly compensated and are truly involved in the process. You'll get the best work from a professional who is fully engaged.

Importantly, ensure the designer assigns your school the copyright in the logo or designs they produce so that you actually own them. This assignment of copyright is often included in the contracts of design professionals, but make sure it's in place, or have an assignment drawn up by a lawyer if you're not using a professional designer.

What is a trade mark?

A trade mark can be word(s), a logo, design, symbol, colour, shape, or sound used to identify a product or service. The words 'Coca-Cola', the Apple logo, and the Nike 'swoosh' are all examples of trade marks.

For our purposes, we'll discuss what makes a good trade mark for a school.

A trade mark should tell the buyer two things: Who is providing a given product or service (i.e. the origin of the goods and services), and — perhaps more importantly — that the provider is associating their name and reputation with the quality and performance of that product or service.

A trade mark protects the public by distinguishing what product or service is provided by whom. This idea of avoiding confusion is at the heart of trade mark law. For example, if you wanted to sell ham sandwiches as McDonald's Ham Sandwiches, you'd likely be denied an Australian trade mark registration and expose yourself to some infringement liability from McDonald's Corporation.

However, if you were opening an accounting practice called McDonald's Tax Prep, you're far less likely to confuse consumers since your accounting service is in a different channel of trade than a fast food restaurant. Of course, McDonald's may still take legal action against your accounting practice.

Types of trade marks

From a technical perspective, there are several categories of potential trade marks.

Generic terms or nouns are not protectable trade marks. For instance, you can't call your school 'Primary School' and hope to trade mark it.

Descriptive names would include someone's name, plus a generic name of their product or service, like 'Brad's Design'. These marks are sometimes more challenging to protect but can be trade marked once they have developed a reputation as a recognisable name for that service.

Suggestive marks may hint at a generic term but take a more creative approach. 'Dunkin' Donuts' is an example.

Arbitrary marks use a word or phrase completely unrelated to the product or service. These marks are often the easiest to protect. Think of Apple, Red Bull, and Target.

Fanciful marks are often made-up words or phrases. They are commonly used with food and beverage brands to allude to the sound or flavour of the food they represent. Think of the sound you hear when you open a can of Pepsi.

What is the role of a trade mark?

One of the most common mistakes organisations make while developing trade marks is trying to use their name or logo to describe what they are, do, or create. As we already mentioned, these descriptive marks are weak trade marks.

Historically, as professional services businesses added new partners, it was not uncommon to add the latest partner's last name to the name of the practice. Over time, this is often reduced to a simplified shorthand of the mark. The same is true of schools.

For example, if Happy Valley Primary School merged with Happy Valley Kindergarten, it might be referred to as 'Happy Valley School' or 'HVS'. If all variations of the trade mark aren't registered, this inconsistent use may begin to weaken the trade mark. In addition, the school could get lost in the alphabet soup. How many school brands can you think of that go by three- or four-letter nicknames?

Of course, there are examples of such shorthands that work very well. IBM, KFC, and UPS are all examples of big corporations that have successfully branded themselves with three-letter trade marks. However, these firms have been in business for decades and have spent millions to help you keep their letters straight. Unless you're planning to spend that kind of money on marketing, you'll probably be better off avoiding a three-letter trade mark altogether.

Let's look at another example. A new school settles on 'Victorian Independent High School' as its brand name and sets its logomark in all black, capital letters in Arial font.

Dr David McCarthy, an Australian registered patent and trade marks attorney, says this is problematic for several reasons.

"First, neither the name nor the design is particularly special. Such a generic trade mark can be very difficult to register with the Australian Trade Marks Office without showing evidence (i) of many years of use of the trade mark (at considerable cost), and to a lesser degree (ii) that the public or potential parents of the school recognise that the name is identifiable specifically with that school. However, it's more likely the name is so ubiquitous that it leaves most of its potential parents in the dark.

"Another problem is that even if you manage to secure your generic trade mark by providing the required evidence of use to the Trade Marks Office, it may not actually be possible in reality to prevent or stop another independent high school in Victoria from referring to their school as a 'Victorian independent high school'. This is because they are able to argue that they are simply describing their location and the services they provide, and not using the phrase as a trade mark. That's why generic trade marks are considered weak. This is aside from the issue that the name can also sound mundane and not the least bit memorable. Think of all of the similarly named schools there might be: Victorian High School, Victorian Independent School, Independent High School of Victoria, etc."

Apple, of course, is the polar opposite of this example. Their logomark is a simple, silhouetted apple design. Neither the brand name nor the mark describes what they do. In fact, the trade mark is based on a fruit — perhaps the farthest thing possible from technology!

However, the name is simple and unexpected for a computer company. The trade mark is also clean and easily recognisable. It works well whether it's large, small, silk-screened or embossed, and across various digital media. What makes the Apple brand engaging goes well beyond the simple trade mark, but the Apple word mark and design mark are the cornerstones of Apple's corporate identity.

Like Apple, you want to shoot for a trade mark that's memorable, distinctive, easy to spell, and fun to say. Practice saying your school name aloud. Does it sound strange? Does it roll trippingly off the tongue? Does it sound like a competing school brand? Does it reflect your school's history or heritage?

A great brand name and trade mark are working hardest for their owners when their only role is to uniquely identify the brand they represent.

What is a logo?

A logo is a combination of words and/or distinctive graphics set in a particular colour, typeface, and orientation that are intended to identify particular goods or services.

The logo is often the cornerstone of the visual identity system for any brand. While some consumer brands may have multiple logos (such as a corporate logo and product or sub-brand logos), we're mainly focusing our recommendations on the qualities of a singular school logo.

In design terms, logotype and logomark are two different things. However, they can both serve as trade marks, either separately or together. Think of Target's bullseye design. The type can be considered the 'logotype', and the design can be considered the 'logomark'. Both may be protected as individual trade marks, but together they are also protected as the combined logo and trade mark.

The late, world-renowned American designer Paul Rand was best known for his iconic logo designs, including UPS, IBM, and ABC (American Broadcasting Corporation). While Rand was famous for his simple, beautiful designs, he was also known for his no-nonsense approach. Speaking to the role of a logo, he said:

"A logo is a flag, a signature, an escutcheon.

A logo doesn't sell (directly), it identifies.

A logo is rarely a description of a business.

A logo derives its meaning from the quality of the thing it symbolises, not the other way around.

A logo is less important than the product it signifies; what it means is more important than what it looks like ... it shows you care."

In short, your trade mark or logo should be less concerned with describing your product or service, and more focused on identifying it.

Armed with these legal basics, how should you get started with creating your school's trade mark?

First things first — do your research. With all the online tools available, there's no excuse for not performing at least a cursory clearance search to make sure something similar isn't being used by someone else. The Australian Trade Mark Register is publicly available for conducting searches of your prospective school name and can be accessed from within the Trade Marks Office (IP Australia) website, ipaustralia.gov.au.

Many logo designers have access to member-supported websites such as LogoLounge, which is an archive of more than 300,000 logos. Even a basic Google search can help uncover potentially similar marks. Considering a scorpion trade mark? Try doing a web search for 'scorpion logos' before you get stung.

Think about your future website domain as well. If you're changing the name or starting a new school, search for available domain names. You'll want to look for available dot edu names, Twitter handles, and more. This is another quick way to figure out if anyone else is using your intended trade mark and, if so, how.

Once you're ready to go beyond a cursory search, your trade marks attorney can do an official trade mark search then advise on and finalise your trade mark for your school name.

Be aware that registering your school name as a business name doesn't automatically mean you will be able to register it as a trade mark. A business name will place you on the Australian Securities & Investments Commission (ASIC) records, but it doesn't confer any rights on your name. Only a registered trade mark can grant you rights to your school name Australia-wide.

What is a visual identity?

Visual identity is everything that visually identifies your brand — logos and trade marks, graphics, images, typefaces, corporate colour schemes, materials, packaging, and textures. In effect, it's a system that creates unity across all your brand's touchpoints; from your logo to your website, to your uniforms and site signage. Most successful brands have a brand guidelines document or a visual identity standards manual that serves as a prescriptive guide for how to create new marketing materials while staying consistent with existing ones.

What makes a good visual identity?

A good identity uniquely identifies your school's goods or services. It needs to be different from the competition, yet familiar enough to be recognised as a particular type of school.

Luckily, you won't exactly be starting from scratch. Your Bold School Brand positioning brief and USP will be valuable guideposts in directing how to approach your visual identity. If you follow the recommendations in the positioning brief, chances are good that the final identity will be authentic. In addition to the 'tone' direction it may provide, an important element to consider is how and where your audience is most likely to interact with and experience your school's brand.

Most schools have plenty of opportunities to do this. They include school uniforms, lecterns, exhibition stands, brochures, umbrellas, letterhead, signage, sports equipment, magazines, pens, advertising, buses, and other visual cues. Your school's logo will be reproduced in multiple formats, from embroidery and silk-screen printing to digital assets and traditional printing.

Taking these points of interaction into account will help guide your team towards any special considerations. Will the identity ever need to be large? Does it need to be very small? Are there any other special considerations, such as one-colour printing or uniform embroidery? We've even been asked to brand horse blankets and rubbish bins!

How to hire the right logo designer

Within the graphic design community, work that pushes the boundaries of style and technique is often celebrated for its beauty and design aesthetics alone. Yet in a world where designers judge the work of other designers, some award-winning pieces may not have been successful in the real world, or at least not yet. Be sure to find a design or branding partner who prioritises your school's goals over their aesthetic preferences. After all, an award-winning visual identity system that's ineffective is not doing its job.

While appropriate style considerations should come into play while thinking about your brand's audience, look for a design partner whose portfolio of work matches your goals. Keep in mind how the identity is most likely to be used and you're more likely to end up with one that's built for performance. As one of Josh's favourite design professors used to say, "The best identity system lets everything reflect unity, not just blind uniformity. Each piece should look like it's part of a family, but the family shouldn't all look like identical twins!"

What should your trade mark look like?

While it should be pretty obvious, this needs to be said: Don't try to cut corners by copying an existing trade mark or logo. Besides the fact that it's unethical and illegal to duplicate another school's intellectual property, the lesser crime of mimicking another school's identity is just not smart. Remember, the goal of your trade mark is to avoid confusion in the marketplace and to uniquely identify your school. Using the same colour, typeface, or concept as your competition or any other popular trade mark is a very poor way to accomplish this.

Above all, you should strive to make your logo original and distinctive.

Sometimes that can be a formidable challenge.

A logo that feels like it belongs in a certain marketplace may be quickly recognised as part of that market but, as such, it's just as likely to blend in and go unnoticed.

Having a logo that's similar to your competition reduces your chances of standing out. A good example is the use of a cross for Christian faith-based schools. It's a powerful identifier, but it's not unique in this context.

Consider embracing distinctive colours, shapes, scale, typography, and styling. While being different may feel uncomfortable at first, you'll be pleased when your logo is the only one to look that way.

Which colours are generally overused by other schools? Which colours do your closest competitors use? Sometimes in very crowded markets, there are few colours that aren't being used, but the range of shades, tints, and combinations of colours should afford you nearly infinite possibilities to stake out a one-of-a-kind colour palette.

Is there a particular colour that you favour, even though it's common? Consider how you could use that colour differently or incorporate complementary colours.

Different styles of logos

From a design perspective, logos can be categorised as follows.

Logotypes: Logotypes, or 'fanciful' marks, are stylised type alone. Think of Coles, David Jones, and Microsoft. Often the most successful logotypes use custom-drawn letterforms, or a typeface that has been somewhat customised for the mark. This prevents other companies from being able to easily duplicate the mark. Logotypes often work best in horizontal formats.

Badges: Badge marks are self-contained marks that are flexible on dark or light fields. They can overlay a photograph and still be readable. Many car manufacturers have badge marks. Think Harley Davidson, Ford, BMW, and Lamborghini. These marks are often circular or square, giving them great prominence on a car hood or television commercial.

Mark and type combo: This is one of the most common styles of logo design. A mark and type logo offers flexibility and can be rearranged in a horizontal or vertical stack. Examples include the ABC (Australian Broadcasting Corporation), Woolworths, and Qantas.

Mark only: Very few brands can stand alone as just a mark. It takes years of exposure and millions of dollars in advertising. These are truly iconic brands like Nike and Apple. Occasionally these marks are used as mark and type combinations, but you're most likely to see them used as mark only.

Do I always have to use my logo the same way?

Consistent usage of your trade mark is paramount. As you can imagine, a logo that's being used inconsistently is much more difficult to protect and enforce. You may also risk losing your trade mark registration for non-use where your trade mark logo is applied differently from what's shown on your trade mark registration.

TM, ®, and proprietary notices

Trade mark rights arise from use and/or registration. Therefore, your mark doesn't have to be registered for you to use proprietary notices like the ™ (trade mark). By using a TM with your school name and/or logo, you're claiming, or 'giving notice', to customers and competitors that you are using your name and/or logo as a trade mark. However, that only provides a minimum level of protection against infringements of your mark under the more difficult to prove common law rights.

The most basic way to formally protect your mark is to apply for a trade mark registration.

To use the registered trade mark symbol, ® (or 'R-Ball' as it's sometimes called), your trade mark must be registered through the Trade Marks Office (IP Australia). Properly maintained, a trade mark registration can last for the life of the product or service. Infringement of a registered trade mark can open the door to a federal court case. When applying for a trade mark registration, you will need to submit:

- Information about the owner of the trade mark.
- A description of the goods and/or services on which the mark is used.
- An image of the mark if it's a logo or 'device' mark.
- The appropriate filing fees for each class of goods or services.

The application process for a trade mark can be long and arduous — the minimum amount of time to registration is seven and a half months. Complex cases can take two years or longer. Registration is not guaranteed. Don't expect anything to happen too quickly, but once you've got a registered trade mark, you have yet another asset for your school and your brand. At this point, you can and should begin using the ® symbol in conjunction with your trade mark.

How can you protect your trade mark?

What's the best way to build and maintain the strength of your trade mark? The first (and most overlooked) step is to use it correctly and consistently in text and marketing materials. Think also about how you can distinguish your trade mark when you're not able to use it in its graphic form. Perhaps it's always in all capital letters, title case, bold face, italics, a certain colour, or different in some other way from the surrounding copy.

You've probably seen brochures, websites, or printed advertisements that show the ® after every mention of a product or service. While this isn't necessarily wrong, it can be disruptive for the reader. It's also legally acceptable to only use the appropriate proprietary symbol once per message or page. Often the first appearance of the trade mark is the most appropriate place to do this. If it's a website, you may choose to give notice once on every page. On a business card, you'd only need to give notice on one side. In a print ad, once is enough.

For further protection, always use your mark as an adjective, not a noun, e.g. 'Xerox copiers' and 'Kleenex facial tissues'. These are two pretty well-known examples of marks that have become increasingly difficult to protect. Xerox and Kleenex are sometimes used as generic terms for copy machines and facial tissues, yet they are both registered trade marks. If your mark becomes generic, you could lose your exclusive rights to your own brand name. For obvious reasons, this is a major pitfall that savvy marketers should avoid.

Standards guides and approval processes

Brand identity standards guides and approval processes are two additional safeguards that, when properly in place, will help protect your trade marks.

At imageseven, we develop a visual identity standards guide for our school branding clients that outlines proper usage of their trade mark, brand colours, typography, and other design elements. For larger schools, we often outline the basic structure of their print collateral templates, email signatures, and the language in their marketing materials.

For logo usage, the most important elements are design, clearance, colours, and applications (including what not to do). For many logos, we show not only the primary usage, but sometimes also include a shorthand or alternative orientation of the logo for special applications. For example, we may design a nickname mark or a vertical version of a long-named, horizontally oriented logo. Of course, we always specify one version that's the preferred mark, so the alternative version is only used for special requirements. Ideally, both forms of your trade mark should be registered. Regardless, be sure the standards guide specifies the design of the logo, including the typeface, and whether it's a standard font or a customised version.

Another important element of consistent usage is logo clearance — the 'safety zone'. Logo clearance is usually measured as a percentage or ratio of an element of a logo. For example, if the logo is a big X, the clearance around all four sides of the logo may be half the height of the X. This ensures that, regardless of how large or small the logo is displayed, it always has the same amount of space around it relative to the size of the logo itself.

Your standards guide should also spell out flexible yet consistent use of colour. Most designers will specify a particular shade of a logo colour using the Pantone Matching System. Pantone colours are communicated as a number and should also include the relative colour name, such as Pantone 288 Blue. Certain Pantone or other spot ink colours may reproduce better across various media than others. Talk with your designer about selecting colours that will both look great as spot colours and convert nicely to a full-colour or four-colour (CMYK) printing process, as well as for on-screen video and web graphics.

Finally, the standards guide should include examples of proper usage of the logo across various media. Some standards will even include how the logo should be 'locked-up' with other graphic page elements such as a tagline, phone number, call to action, or web address. Examples of what not to do should also be included, such as colour shifting, rotating, distorting, manipulating, ghosting, or placing a logo over a dark or busy image.

Regardless of how loose or strict your usage policies may be, they won't help protect your brand if nobody is enforcing them. Select someone to sign off on all newly created materials, or at least have several staff members share in the review process. An ideal approval process should include a simple checklist of do's and don'ts to maintain brand consistency.

Last but not least, it's essential that your school police the marketplace to ensure no one is violating your trade mark/s. You may never need to go much further than a phone call or email, but a simple 'cease and desist' letter from your trade mark attorney can be an invaluable next line of defence. At the very least, don't allow violations of your trade mark to persist, or it will demonstrate indirectly that you're okay with the violation, which will decrease the strength of your rights moving forward.

Be advised

Understanding all that goes into a professionally designed logo and visual identity system underscores our caution against using a friend or ambitious amateur to develop some of the most valuable assets of your brand. Do you think your neighbour or brother-in-law will do a more than cursory search or know how to properly assemble a visual identity standards guide?

With all the potential issues that may arise from a new identity system — aesthetically, strategically, and legally — weigh your options heavily before cutting corners in this phase of brand development.

Case study: Imitation is not flattery, it's theft

imageseven was engaged to protect the intellectual property (IP) for this international, single sex, PreK–12, high-fee day and boarding school.

The school had never paid attention to protecting their IP but as their brand became stronger and more well-known, they increasingly found that other schools were seeking to imitate them.

On one level, it was flattering but, for a school with global reach, it was important to remain distinctive from other schools. Like many schools, they had a name that was similar to those in other states and countries. Confusion on the part of a prospective parent was a very real possibility, even if there was no intent to copy our client.

The school's visual identity comprised their formal school crest (complex) and an informal 2D mascot (simple) derived from an element in the crest, which was used on sports uniforms and merchandise. They also had their formal name (long) and their common name (short).

The crest had been trade marked many years previously. The 2D mascot was deemed generic and could not be trade marked on its own. However, the mascot with the school name (logo and typography) could be protected so we organised this. Taglines were also examined and protected.

The school now keeps an active watch on potential breaches of their trade marks.

Insight applied

- IP protection always seems expensive at the time, but the effects are long-lasting.
- When you need to resort to a trade mark for protection, it's too late to start thinking about the process, which frequently takes more than six months.
- It's common that a school name alone is considered too generic for a successful trade mark application, but the combination of your school logo with the particular typography of your visual identity has a much greater chance of being protected.
- Trade marks can be useful protection for very simple matters such as a local embroidery firm that produces cheap and off-brand imitation blazers when the school is attempting to keep consistency. When denied the ability to embroider the blazer pocket, the firm's incentive to imitate will be removed.

CHAPTER EIGHT

Collateral, campaigns, and content: Brand touchpoints that work best for schools

How to determine and prioritise the most appropriate methods.

If you need a loan, chances are that your bank will ask for something to use as collateral. For them, collateral is like an insurance policy, showing them you're as good as your word.

Perhaps you've never thought of it this way, but marketing collateral isn't all that different. Collateral is a validation tool that helps back up the story of your school's capabilities. Even great collateral isn't ever going to take the place of face-to-face conversations between your enrolment team and prospective school parents, but it can help parents leave those meetings with a sense of security that lasts beyond the conversation. It should echo your brand messages and be consistent with your visual identity and brand standards.

Working out what you need

It used to be a given in school marketing that every parent would start off by declaring, "I need a brochure." Of course, a brochure or prospectus is seldom the best way to solve a marketing problem. Today, it's far more common for parents to ask for something digital — a website, Twitter account, or social media address.

The tools may have changed, but the questions remain the same. For example, does your school really need a Twitter account? Maybe, but how do you determine what to do first? More importantly, how can you decide exactly what you need?

There's no shortage of options. Your school will likely discuss the merits of creating business cards, letterhead, additional stationery pieces, brochures, and other printed material. You may consider advertising campaigns and brand touchpoints, such as signage, apparel, vehicle graphics, exhibition (expo) materials, direct mail, and merchandise. The list of promotional items can be overwhelming — hats, umbrellas, car stickers, pens, and on, and on, and on.

Intimidated? Don't freak out just yet.

Depending on how large your school is, you may only realistically need a few of these items. If it's on the large side, in startup mode, or has a hefty outbound marketing approach, you may need far more. Carefully consider the purpose of each piece before you begin cranking them out. Just because you have the budget to print 10,000 pocket folders doesn't mean you'll use 10,000 of them.

Take a step back to carefully consider what collateral your school really does need. How can you do that?

The two approaches we've found most helpful in prioritising marketing collateral needs are:

- Marketing priorities
- Enrolment opportunities.

That's probably not a shocking list. Most collateral needs stem from items your marketing team feels are missing or information that could help fill a gap in your enrolment process.

Marketing priorities

Start by making a list. Detail every possible marketing collateral need you have. After you've created the list, rank every item as either a '1' (essential today), a '2' (soon to be required), a '3' (not essential but could eventually be helpful), or '4' (basically a luxury, unnecessary for now). Then reorder the list so you can see which items you need to address now, and which items can wait.

Enrolment opportunities

Next, slice up your marketing collateral needs by considering the various stages prospective school parents and their children go through in your enrolment process (include your marketing and enrolment teams in this exercise). For most schools, the stages are probably something like this — unqualified prospect, qualified lead, converted to enrolment, current parent and referral source.

Your method of ranking and qualifying your parental life cycle may differ from this, and that's okay. In fact, it's important to frame this conversation in a way your team will relate to, so adjust the number of stages and labels accordingly. If you haven't categorised prospective parents in this way before, the number of stages or names isn't important. Just try to keep it simple. Understand that they may need different tools and more customised messaging in each stage in order to mature into enrolments.

For instance, early stage opportunities are often more interested in marketing that excites and inspires. What tools would help you accomplish this?

Other categories, especially late stage opportunities, require more face-to-face time and reassurance tactics. What marketing tools would be most helpful in this instance?

Don't forget past and current parents and students. Which marketing tools or tactics would better engage them? It's probably not your brochure.

Now list your opportunities by stage. This should be similar to your marketing priorities list. Consider which stages are likely to be most impacted by the addition of these tools.

Compare your two lists. Which items appear to be your top priorities? The biggest win will come from identifying items that are most requested by marketing and are also items the enrolment team could benefit from. Weigh the potential outcomes of doing a few expensive pieces versus several more affordable items.

At this point, you should have a solid roadmap of which items need top billing and which pieces can wait until later.

Collateral best practice

It would be nearly impossible to write up suggestions for every conceivable piece of collateral. And really, who wants to read that book?

Although each situation is different and the opportunities vary, we do see common patterns among our school clients regarding their collateral needs. Let's look at some of the most common items discussed.

Colour: Across myriad printing options, and the various materials and media, colour can be an incredibly tricky thing to control. We'll assume that you have standardised your school's colours as designated Pantone Matching System numbers, but that's often not enough to ensure consistency.

Have you ever picked out the perfect paint colour for your home only to see that it didn't look quite the same once you slathered it on the wall? Paint colour has a funny way of shifting based on the surroundings, the lighting in the space, and the surface to which it's applied. Printing inks are very much the same. And with colour printers getting cheaper every day, many schools are tempted to print their collateral in-house. This comes with its own set of colour-matching issues.

So while you may have a standard set of Pantone colours in your identity, it always helps to have a sample piece that your printing company can use for matching. Much like those home improvement store paints, your printer can adjust colour mixes to better dial in the perfect shade of your Pantone colour. Don't be afraid to ask!

An experienced designer will go out of their way to help you with this, because it can be pretty embarrassing to have a portfolio full of mismatched print samples. Ask for suggestions for spot colours and any other processes you plan to pursue. Having unique colour mixes specified for coated versus uncoated paper stock can be a huge help too. In addition, Pantone Australia sells a Colour Bridge Set that demonstrates how well certain colours translate from spot to process printing. Keep an eye out for potential problems from the start and insist on colours that perform well across all media.

Consistency: Outside matching colours, consistency in design, rhythm, language, and texture are all things your prospective and actual school parents are likely to respond to. Resist the urge to switch things up on every other piece you develop. If you find yourself bored by your brand consistency, remember that members of your target audience don't see the collateral every day like you do, so don't assume they are getting bored too. As we discussed earlier, strive to reflect unity, not blind uniformity.

Business cards: For most schools, business cards are ascribed with more value than they have. Special paper stocks, inks and die-cuts will seldom win you another enrolment. Few people within a school beyond the Head, the Admissions Director and the Director of Development will have use for a business card. However, these cards are often seen as validation of a role. So they can't be noticeably cheap and nasty, but neither should they be obsessed over.

Business cards are also prime territory for brand inconsistency to creep in. Enforce strict compliance with the template outlined in your brand's visual style guide. When the Head and a member of the executive hand over cards that are different because they were printed at different times, on different paper stocks, and with slightly different designs, it reflects poorly on the education product the school will deliver.

Stationery package: Don't be afraid to consider different types of papers and specialty printing processes to help differentiate your stationery package. As many schools have forgone printing paper stationery altogether, an elegantly designed and printed piece stands out that much more.

Brochures and other print collateral: Do you really need a brochure? Think through any proposed print item and consider if it's something you just think you're supposed to do, or if it will be an asset that will actually get some use. Also, consider at what stage in the admissions and enrolment process a brochure would be most useful and tailor the messaging to that stage.

Schools exhibition displays, presentation kits, and PowerPoint templates: What do these three things have in common? In our experience, they usually have too much copy and other unnecessary elements crammed into the space. Treat each of them like a billboard. Use fewer words, more sizzle, and memorable concepts!

Presentation materials are common in schools marketing, but they're usually accompanied by a presenter. Don't try to tell the whole story with these pieces. Be sure to leave something to the imagination. Don't try to communicate everything at once.

Ad specialties, apparel, and other gear: Similar to your expo display or PowerPoint template, your school's promotional items should aim to do more with less. A classy logo and URL on your school umbrella or polo shirt is probably not only better looking but is far more likely to be used or worn than something featuring a corny marketing message.

Vehicle graphics, billboards, and other ads: Do you remember the last time you wrote down a phone number you saw on a billboard? Or called the school whose phone number appeared on the bus in front of you? You're wasting an opportunity to provide useful information on a billboard or vehicle if you're listing a giant phone number. There are very few exceptions. Seriously, unless you have integrated it deeply into your branding, lose the phone number on your vehicles and billboards.

Instead, view billboards and fleet graphics as canvasses on which to echo your brand message or location. Location billboards are highly effective. Vehicle graphics with calls to action? Not so much.

Other touchpoints: Lastly, remember that every touchpoint you have with a staff member, supplier, parent, student, other stakeholder, or the wider community is an opportunity to express your brand message or promote your current campaign.

Don't fall into the trap of: "Oh, it's just a parking lot sign — it doesn't have to be that professional." Wrong.

Think about the last time you encountered an unexpected but well-executed brand touchpoint. Perhaps it was a thank you card, a professional-looking school report, an event program, or a prospectus. What did it make you think about that school?

Let's take a look at the business card that Sally Hogshead uses. She's a renowned keynote speaker and personal branding consultant. Her business card is oversized, colourful and interactive. The seven strips on her card reveal messages that relate to her consulting practice and it's very nicely designed.

"Once you fascinate someone, they become totally focused on your message. So when we were creating our business card for Fascinate, Inc., of course it needed to fascinate people," Sally says. "This business card is an invitation to interact. It immediately captures attention ... people love seeing which trigger best describes their personality, hidden underneath that peel-off strip."

Campaigns

If you're considering an advertising campaign, regardless of whether it's print, television, outdoor, or online, you need to remember two things:

- Most people are trying to ignore your interruption tactics as much as possible.
- Unless it's really clear what you want someone to remember and do, they probably won't remember or do anything.

Look-alike, sound-alike, and me-too messaging in your advertising is a tremendous waste of valuable advertising dollars. You're better off spending zero dollars on advertising than blowing money on imitation messaging.

Remember, your advertising campaigns can change seasonally or annually. Ad campaigns give you freedom to push the expression of your brand within the bounds of your brand standards, but ensure they stay within the visual identity guidelines for consistency.

Get creative and come at it from a different angle. If you don't, nobody is going to remember your brand, and certainly not your offer or campaign. Remember, be different, not corny.

Visually speaking, campaigns give you an opportunity to dress up the brand in something new without completely throwing away your brand standards. Aldi,

Apple, and iiNet are just some of the companies that do campaigns impeccably well. Always fresh, yet always on point.

It's true that in the commercial world, many companies are pulling money from traditional advertising and using those dollars for SEO marketing, social media, and other content marketing opportunities. Whether that makes sense for your situation depends on the factors surrounding your school.

Content marketing

One of the hottest areas for school marketers and leaders today is content marketing.

Content marketing is the practice of creating valuable content to help tell your brand's story. It uses news stories, articles, how-to pieces, testimonials, blogs, white papers, case studies, videos, infographics, ebooks, and more.

Every school now has the opportunity to be the leading informational expert on their area of education 24 hours a day by providing the most compelling and relevant content online to their target audience. Who knew that publishing could be the ultimate competitive advantage for schools?

Going back to old-school Marketing 101, marketing activities are classified as using either push or pull tactics. Push tactics interrupt a person and try to get them to do something. Pull tactics, in the traditional sense, are things that draw a person in, like a sale or event. Today, pull tactics include relationship building, conversational tactics, and becoming a trusted resource for your market.

Content marketing definitely fits best under this updated view of pull marketing. And one of the great things about it is that many expressions of content marketing only require your time. Unlike ad campaigns or pay-per-click marketing, it's often a very inexpensive approach to generating new leads.

Content marketing is valuable in many ways. Let's look at three.

1. **It's real**

   It helps humanise your school's brand and forces you to have a content-producing mindset. When you're developing content regularly, your voice is going to be heard. It's tough to put every piece of content being developed through the same filters that an ad might go through.

2. It's often real-time

Tweets, live blogging on your school website, and video streaming on social media (e.g. Facebook Live) give you an opportunity to respond to real-world events and industry news stories as they happen.

3. It takes real thinking

If you were pressed to write down everything you knew about a particular topic in an hour, the task would be very intimidating at first. By the end of the hour, you would probably have lost track of time. The reality is that you're probably much more knowledgeable in your area of expertise than you realise. Content marketing provides an outlet for sharing that knowledge. Demonstrating your depth of knowledge is often referred to as thought leadership.

Where to start building content marketing

With content marketing as a mindset, it's easy to find the benefits but tough to find the starting line. We recommend starting with a small yet foundational content marketing strategy that's within the grasp of nearly every school: Blogging.

The word 'blog' comes from the original idea of a web log or online journal. Eventually, users shortened it to blog. A blog is a website (or section within a site) that has serial content — you add to it whenever you like — and it's all kept in one place.

Most basic blogging platforms are free to use, but you may need someone a bit more technical to help you get it set up and looking the way you want. WordPress, Blogger, and Tumblr are just a few options.

If you're working with a content marketing team and are ready for a more advanced tool than one of the free options, consider investing in a content marketing system (CMS). WordPress, for example, offers tools such as content calendars, greater administrative controls, and ways to capture student stories.

A blog is a great place to originate content for use in other places and/or to tease with deeper content that you may have produced as a book, PDF, or white paper. You can use the same content that appears on your blog in enewsletters, brochures, print advertisements, and more.

Here are three great ways blogging can work for your school.

1. Blogging is an inexpensive way to begin to develop your content marketing muscles. Writing about what you know helps you develop your school's brand voice and deepens your own understanding of that topic.

2. It's social. Blogging doesn't have to be limited to people who intentionally plan to visit your blog. You can share blog posts by linking to them in your email signature and through social media, which we'll discuss in greater depth in chapters ten and eleven. You can also enable a function that allows visitors to comment. Seek bloggers you respect and begin commenting on their blogs as well. Chances are that you'll see an uptick in traffic and comments on your own blog as a result.

3. Blogging is the gateway to other types of content marketing. Depending on your blogging platform, you can post photo galleries, LinkedIn SlideShare posts, videos, infographics, and links to other content platforms such as Instagram, all from your blog. As your blogging efforts grow, so do your content marketing opportunities!

So get blogging and remember: Every touchpoint is an opportunity to show just how professional your school brand is. Make the most of every one, be it collateral, campaign, or content.

Case study: Prioritising and standardising content

A statewide system of primary and secondary schools looked to imageseven for help with implementing a campaign to lift awareness and generate enrolment enquiries.

The system of schools, although well-known in their state, had not done any combined marketing for many years. Until this point, all marketing had been executed at a local school level.

The new program was to be both a marketing test and a positioning exercise to convey diversity of opportunity within the system. The budget was limited, reflecting the scale of the test.

The execution that the client settled on was a combination of collateral, weighted towards Out-of-Home advertising (such as billboards and shopping centre digital advertising), television, and regional press. The intent was to drive people to the website, where they could engage with specific online content, e.g. video, articles, and downloads for specific schools. Website visitors were then invited to fill in an enquiry form and were followed up in person.

The results were impressive:

- Nearly 600 enrolment interactions
- 225,000 website page views
- 1.3 million social media views
- Over one million Out-of-Home views.

Insight applied

- School salespeople (enrolments staff, admissions teams, registrars, and even Heads) are often more comfortable with something to hand out than with talking to a prospective family.
- Before approving a new piece of collateral, ask when and where it will be used, and how. Wherever possible, it might be replaced by a personal conversation or a piece of online information to which prospects might be referred to back up a conversation.
- Schools spend significant resources generating enrolment leads. When one of them takes the trouble to make contact (phone, email, or visit), make the time to talk to them. Marketing generates leads. People make sales.
- Individual schools seldom have the budgetary resources to run true campaigns. Consider thinking of them as brand themes that might run for a year, or even two.

Brand impact

> **"**
>
> Beautiful, unique, and well-designed brands can't exist in vacuums. The most amazing strategies and well-executed designs in the world are completely worthless if they fail to accomplish goals, grow a movement, or yield results.
>
> Your school brand's touchpoints are the individual interactions and tactics that you can leverage to engage with prospective families, maximising the user experience.
>
> In this section, we'll explore recommendations for website design, social media, and digital marketing.

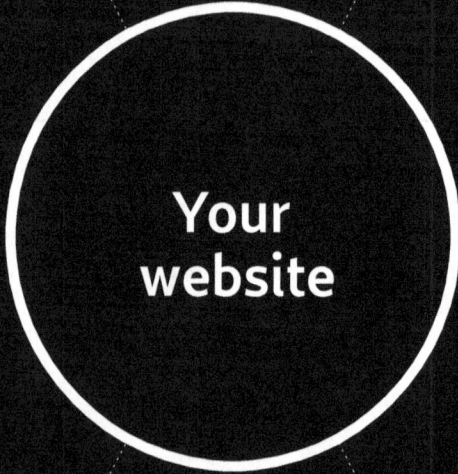

Facebook

Instagram

Your
website

LinkedIn

Blog

CHAPTER NINE

Websites and digital media: Identifying the hub of your Bold School Brand

When it comes to attracting enrolments, where should you start online, and which digital platform should be the hub of your brand?

Where do you start?

Once you've developed your new visual identity, the next step is to begin applying your new look and feel to your school's website and other online properties.

There aren't any magic levers, but your web presence is likely the most effective validation tool available. So your website should be the digital reflection of the brand you've worked so hard to develop. The messages, images, videos, and articles should echo and reinforce your brand's voice.

As such, your website will be an invaluable resource as a validation tool. Prospective school parents visiting it will quickly digest who you are, what you're about, and why they should care. And best of all, the impression they get from your website will reinforce what the marketplace has already told them about your school. When they perceive that level of consistency, they'll experience a high level of comfort in their ability to trust your school to solve their education problems.

Your website should also be a highly efficient enrolment tool. It should not only be a destination for prospective families but capture casual visitors and turn them into promising leads for your enrolment team.

Is that how you would describe your website?

Ask yourself the following:

- Is our website looking a little dated?
- Does our enrolments team use it as a marketing tool?
- Is our messaging differentiated from our competition?
- Do we know how many leads are coming from our website? If we do know, is the answer zero?

Maybe you know your website isn't cutting it. Take heart! It's not just you. This problem exists with many schools. We call this a 'website emergency'.

Is your school facing a website emergency?

While the redesign of your website may be the next logical step in the branding process as we've described it so far, most clients ask us to fix their website first. In fact, we like to joke that imageseven's conference room has become a makeshift triage station for marketing patients! For the many reasons we've already discussed, websites seem to be the most common marketing emergency we encounter.

If we asked 100 schools if their websites were under the weather or worse, nearly half of them would say yes.

An ill-performing website can be the symptom of a larger positioning problem rather than the problem itself. But that doesn't change the fact that these websites are presenting some serious symptoms.

Luckily for you, if you've been following the book so far, you now have a much tighter handle on positioning. So whether you're redesigning your website to better reflect your school's brand or you're building it for the first time, here are the top ten things, by category, we recommend avoiding.

Content emergencies

It's often easy to spot a dated look or a site that doesn't perform well on mobile devices, but content problems can be tougher to identify. Here are the top content-related issues we regularly combat.

1. It's all about you

Does your site inspire visitors with compelling messages and fantastic photography? Does it offer them what they're looking for, or does it focus on your school's history and go on and on about your mission?

Think about why you take the time to view another school's website. When was the last time you surfed around wanting to read its mission statement?

Which pages are most important from a content standpoint? Historically, the most visited pages on a school website are the homepage, about us, contact, and tuition fees. Blogs may not be your most trafficked pages today, but if optimised for search engines, they can easily surpass your homepage in total visits and time on page.

2. Ignoring the value

Most schools are highly relationship driven. Not just online relationships, but real, human relationships. That's a great thing, but it's not an excuse to have a dated, less than professional website. Your present parents may excuse your sub-par site, but they're not your only potential visitors.

Your website's number one opportunity is to serve as a validation tool for prospective school parents and future students. These visitors don't have the benefit of an existing relationship with you. Your website may be the first impression they develop of your school.

And it's not just about parents. Many of our school clients have stated that their investment in a new website was driven by a need to attract and appeal to top teaching staff.

3. Poor-quality content and photography

If your photos and website copy don't hold your attention, they surely won't impress anyone else. Spend some quality time on what you're saying, and only show off your best work. If the photos or other pieces of content aren't showing your school at its best, get rid of them.

As we described earlier regarding The Scots College, Sydney (NSW), quality photography can play a major role in branding. Finding a photographer who can support and build your brand is a wise investment.

4. Stale content

Evergreen content is great, but you should strive to give visitors a reason to keep coming back. Search engines love fresh content too. Does your site still say © 2015 or worse? One practical fix for this problem is to build your website on a platform or CMS that allows you to make simple text, photo and other content updates on the fly, without the assistance of your IT department or web designer.

Ideally, you should be adding to or updating your content regularly. But perhaps things at your school don't change very often. What should you update in that case? Consider adding a blog. Many school Heads have an aversion to the word blog, but usually they're picturing the wrong thing.

Your school's blog isn't the place for posting lightweight content. It should position you as thought leaders and answer questions that prospective families want to ask.

At the very least, schedule a regular time to update your website, such as once a month. Think about updating news stories or blogs, or reviewing your extra-curricular offerings. Have you held any events recently? Has your school been in the news? Is there anything outdated that should be removed?

5. One-way communication

Are you providing avenues for feedback or conversation? What's your call to action? Including blogs, videos, and links to social media are great tactics to consider.

Do whatever makes sense for your school, but don't limit conversation with your website's visitors by just using static text.

Design emergencies

Obviously, the design of your site should be in line with your new visual identity standards, taking full advantage of your unique positioning, voice, and look. However, here are a few factors to be aware of.

6. Not responsive

A recent imageseven study of Australian independent school websites found that 46 percent were not optimised for mobile. Yet, without a doubt, responsive web design is one of the biggest recent changes to how websites are being built.

If you're not familiar with this approach, responsive sites allow the layout, content, navigation, and other features to adjust, scale, move, or respond based on the screen size of the visitor's device. To put that another way, schools leveraging responsive design can deliver an optimised experience to visitors, regardless of whether they're using desktop, laptop, tablet, or mobile phone devices. In addition, responsive websites enable school marketers to manage their website content for all devices in one place — no more updating the desktop version then updating the mobile version.

Responsive design expands far beyond making a site mobile-friendly. It's also about how the code is written and organised. Consideration should be made for offering multiple image sizes for various devices, retina displays, and slower connection speeds. Responsive sites are lightweight and load quickly on mobile devices, even with slower internet connections.

Each of these tactics not only speeds up your site's performance but decreases your long-term site maintenance costs. Also, because they are accessible to more people (including those with poor internet connections and people with disability), Google is playing favourites when it comes to sites that are optimised for mobile viewing, so your mobilised site should rank higher.

With more and more traffic originating on mobile devices, website designs are increasingly being considered from a mobile perspective first, with those design considerations driving the desktop experience.

If you're planning to redesign your website, don't do it until you're ready to invest in a responsive website.

7. What do you want me to do?

Calls to action are marketing speak for the graphics or messages throughout your site that invite visitors to take a next step. You might want them to read more, fill out a form, download a PDF, or pick up the telephone. Many schools work hard to send traffic to their websites, but how many consider what they want the visitor to do once they get there?

For each audience group that visits your website — prospective parent or student, competitor school, potential teacher, casual visitor — what's your goal? What would you want each of them to do when they land on your homepage or blog post? Get inspired? Contact you? Sign up for your newsletter? Many websites fall short when it comes to calls to action or moving visitors through the site. Make sure that what you want the visitor to do is clear to them.

8. Elevate your people and your process

In the past, many schools may have been a little skittish to feature their key staff for the world to see. "What if someone tries to poach my best teachers?" But in a world where your best staff are already on LinkedIn and other social networks, there is far more benefit to allowing prospective parents to 'meet' your team on the website first as it goes a long way towards demonstrating your school's expertise.

SEO emergencies

SEO is the practice of helping a website rank higher for a particular search term. The following are very basic optimisation tips, but still a good place to start if you're new to SEO.

9. Invisible to search engines

Google your school or your category and market (e.g. Brisbane independent primary schools). Did you find your school on the first page? No? Well, neither did your prospective family.

SEO refers to the ongoing efforts of sending search traffic to your website for the right reasons, and the science of optimising your website to be found for specific searches.

The first may require ongoing consultation, but the latter is essential to take into account as you build your new site. If you understand nothing else about SEO, the key is very simple: Be consistent. A page on your site with a keyword found in the page name, title, headline, and body copy is far more likely to rank for that keyword than a page that is inconsistent. As Google's focus on mobile continues to grow, SEO and responsive web design will go hand-in-hand to improve search rankings.

10. Nobody is keeping score

How many visitors does your site average each month? What's the most popular content on your site? What search terms do visitors use to locate your website? How do visitors find you? If you're not checking your statistics, you'll never know.

Most hosting companies provide free access to these statistics. If yours doesn't, spend a few minutes adding Google Analytics or a similar analytics package to your site. Many are free and they'll provide you with data on traffic, visitors, length of visits, and much more.

Make an effort to review web analytics at least once a month to determine if your activity over the past month has yielded any results.

The website leadership emergency

Sometimes the biggest challenge is deciding who will take ownership of the website from a marketing perspective. That person will need to make ongoing decisions about how often to make updates, how to drive more traffic, and how to convert that traffic into qualified leads.

Sometimes this role is filled by a member of staff and other times it's an outside consultant. Either way, the website needs someone to own it.

If you're reading this book, the best person for this job is probably you. Congratulations!

Eliminating website emergencies: How to go from bad to bold

So how do we overcome these challenges? How can your school develop a web presence that's consistent with your new brand strategy and drives enrolment leads?

To drive leads, you must first drive engagement. Engagement goes beyond mere visits. Engagement means your visitors are interacting with your site, reading content, requesting information, sharing your site with friends, or coming back regularly. Engaged visitors are potential school parents and students, future staff, and sometimes your peers.

What does it take to get visitors engaged with your brand online?

There are four levels of online brand engagement.

1. Be found

If a website wins an award in the forest and no one is there to click on it, does it still generate leads?

Consider this very real problem. If you have the greatest school in the country, yet no one visits your site or knows how to get there, it's not a very effective website.

There are several reasons why websites can't be found. Perhaps the architecture makes it difficult for it to be identified by search engines. Or maybe the site isn't being marketed very well, if at all. But the bottom line is, being found is the very first level of engagement for your school's brand online.

2. Pass the two-second test

Most websites are allowed about two seconds to demonstrate they're the site the searcher was looking for. Otherwise they move on.

Think about the last time you searched for something you knew little about. You entered the search phrase. Hit go. Scanned the list. Clicked on the first item — and within two seconds or less, you made the decision to either dig deeper or hit the back button to further your search.

When a website passes the two-second test, it usually has one or more of the following qualities: captivating headlines, images, or design; obvious placement of keywords; or an easily recognisable, branded look.

When a visitor finds your site, does it pass the two-second test? The surest way to determine that is to review your website analytics. Pay particular attention to the time on page and bounce rate, which can both be indicative of search behaviour. Bounce rate is the percentage of visitors who visit your site and quickly hit the back button. Search engines appear to diminish results for sites with higher bounce rates.

3. Invite users to dig deeper

Let's say your site passes the two-second test. Now what?

It should provide enough valuable information to encourage the visitor to dig deeper. Whether your point of view is something every visitor will agree with or your philosophy rings true isn't the point. Not everyone will be a qualified lead.

But does your site at least get them deep enough that they can begin to qualify themselves?

How do you measure this? Again, take a look at your website analytics. Consider the number of pages per visit and average time on site.

4. Drive visitors to take action

Comfy chairs, convenient locations, free wi-fi ... these are all great reasons to visit your local coffee shop. However, those coffee shop owners didn't set up shop for their neighbours to hang out with them. Their goal is to sell coffee.

Sometimes websites end up doing something similar. These sites may draw thousands of visits per month yet yield no immediate action.

So keep this in mind: Once your site is found, passes the two-second test, and encourages the visitor to dig deeper, the final goal is to get them to act.

What's your call to action? Better yet, what constitutes action online? For every school, it's probably a little different, but here are some of the most common types of action: click here to learn more, send an email, fill out a form, make a phone call, subscribe to an email newsletter, or download a prospectus. Beyond the more traditional online calls to action are social calls to action. These include clicking through to something, becoming a fan, following, friending, subscribing to a blog or podcast, tweeting, forwarding to a friend, and other types of social sharing.

First things first

One of the most overlooked considerations in redesigning a website is determining what you want visitors to do once they arrive.

They are here, but now what?

Perhaps the main thing you want them to do is on your homepage. But is it obvious? Here's a hint: If everything is bold, italic, caps, red, or big on your page, it's all fighting for prominence. If everything looks important, nothing will stand out on its own.

How do you get the important details to stand out from the rest?

To begin, think about the hierarchy of each element on your homepage. List the five most important. Perhaps it looks something like this:

1. Who are we? Logo, name, etc.
2. What do we do? We specialise in a particular area of education.
3. Call to action. Click here to download a prospectus.
4. Contact information. How to reach us or connect online.
5. Navigation. Here's how to explore further.

Your list may be longer than five items and certainly may be in a different order, but try this exercise first to determine what's most important on the page. Next, think about the less important elements that also belong on the homepage. Lastly, cut any elements that are not necessary to have on the page at all. If possible, do this for every page.

Now express this list of hierarchy visually. We call these wireframes. It's a simple activity that you can do on a whiteboard. Draw boxes that represent each element on the page. Repeat this process for your mobile experience as well.

Which element is most important visually? Is that reflected both in your ordered list and your wireframe? Great! Now you can use these wireframes to design a more successful, responsive website.

In the end, the importance of each element should translate to the visual hierarchy of the finished website design. And of course, test out different theories. If you think a red button may drive more clicks than the old blue button, test it out with a few people and see if your theory holds true. Unlike a brochure, a website never goes to print, so you can make infinite tweaks, seeking to constantly improve the overall user experience.

Your website is just one of many online tactics you'll likely consider. There are also blogs, social media, email marketing, landing pages, and more.

Which online tactics should you explore first?

It's easy to be overwhelmed by all the online tools that schools can choose from today. So how do you determine and prioritise which tactics to pursue and which to ignore?

Well, what's your strategy? We had a client wonder aloud if their Facebook followers should select their next logo. We thought that was a scary proposition. Unless your strategic plan includes leaving everything to chance, having your social media followers determine major marketing decisions is the opposite of strategy.

It's no different when it comes to determining which online media to pursue. Your strategy should drive your decisions.

Is your strategy to be top of mind with friends and family of potential students across the country, or with local high-net-worth individuals who might become school supporters? Your answers to these types of questions will help you determine if it makes sense to have an engaging Facebook page or to focus on being featured in websites that report on local news.

What is your hub?

As with an airline, having one primary location to run traffic to and from helps simplify your school's ability to maintain an online presence. Identifying your online hub is a major step towards carving out your online brand strategy.

Let's say you decide to elevate your school website to be the hub of your brand. In short, that means the goal of subsequent actions online should be to drive

Facebook   LinkedIn   Blog   Apps   Twitter

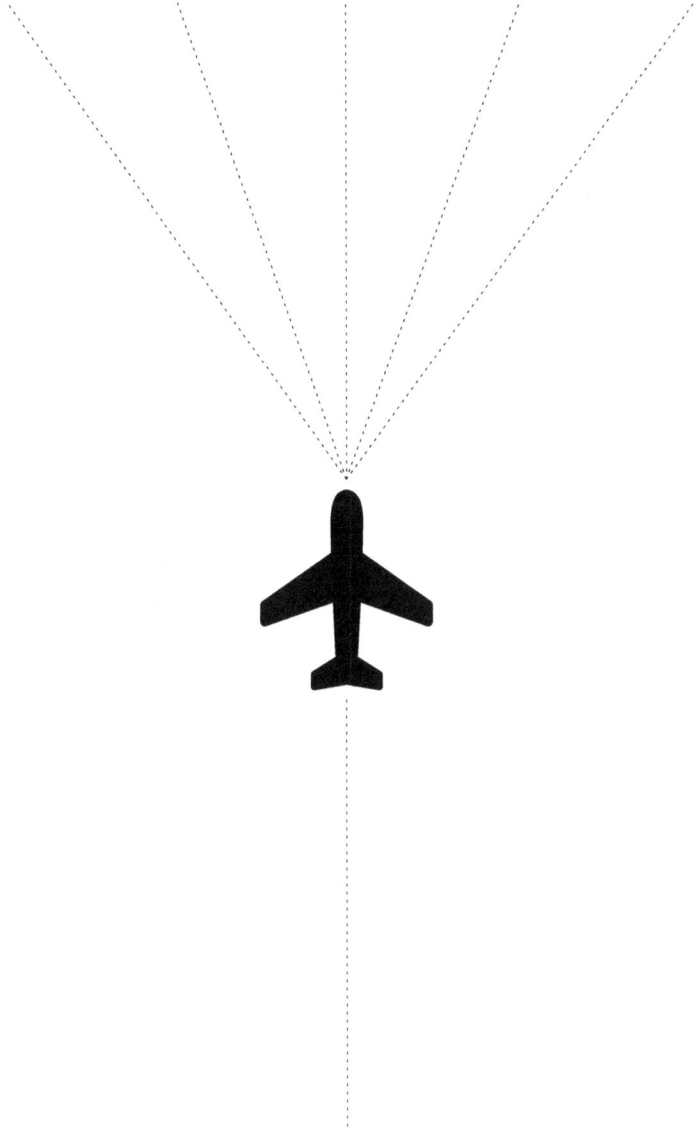

visitors to your website. Whether you're sending out an email marketing message, sponsoring a display ad, tweeting, or posting to your Facebook page, you should primarily be driving visitors to your website.

Of course, every message shouldn't just overtly scream CLICK HERE! But as a rule, think about driving traffic back to your brand hub (in most cases, this will be your primary website).

Another benefit of identifying your hub is that it will help you determine what other online tools you'd like to have and when they should be developed. If you currently have a dated website, no blog, no apps, and no social networks, don't despair. If you're confused about where your hub is supposed to be, go back to your strategy document. Once you're able to develop and maintain your hub at a respectable level, you can move on to additional tactics that will expand your reach.

Remember, if you don't have time to make each endeavour as high-quality as you and your visitors expect it to be, you're not ready to develop it. Whether it's a blog, a Facebook page, or getting started on Instagram, do each to the best of your ability or wait until you're fully ready to start working on them.

How SEO can help your positioning

Another important consideration is how your school ranks with search engines. Most new parents start their enrolment decision journey by using a search engine. If your school is not visible during these searches, you're going to miss out on getting in on early enrolment discussions.

Also consider this: If your school is highly specialised, wouldn't it be natural for it to come up in a search for that specialty?

Take a few minutes to brainstorm search phrases for which you'd like to be found. Think about how you would word these phrases, and how prospective families might word them differently. For example, you might say 'independent school Victoria' and your prospective parent might type 'which is the best private school in Melbourne?'

After you document these terms, type them into your favourite SEO tool or search engine, without being logged in to any Google products (Gmail or Google Analytics, for example). Which schools come up on the first and second page for each? Are you anywhere to be found? What does this tell you?

Imagine, all your hard work to differentiate and position your school, only to have it fail at SEO. Good SEO should harmonise your branding, positioning, website, and other touchpoints.

If it's not something your school has paid attention to in the past, maybe it's time to take a look.

Beyond search

There are many ways to drive traffic to your website outside search engines. You can market your URL using traditional offline methods, include links in your email signatures, and promote your website via social media. Just the thought of committing to social media as a marketing channel is scary for many schools, and we'll address those fears in the next two chapters. For now, begin to explore all the potential you have for getting your website in front of the right people.

Case study: Upgrading the website to increase interest

The client was a regional, co-ed, Year 7-12, low-fee day and boarding school that needed to address lack of interest from prospective parents.

Our early assessment showed this was one of a few non-government school options in the region. As such, it should have been attracting more enquiries than it was.

The prospective parents were spread across a wide geographic area and many would not have firsthand knowledge of the school. The website was its shopfront but had been built in the early days of the school by the town's resident graphic designer, photographer, web developer, and marketing consultant … which were all the same person.

The site design was unprofessional and outdated. The imagery was unattractive, didn't show the school's best features, and the featured students weren't in consistent uniform.

Content was thin and only addressed points of comparison with the government school competition. It didn't address the many points of difference and advantages that were inherently part of the school's offering.

There was also no attempt to engage with the prospective parent, with only an email address as a point of contact. There was no call to action.

In many ways, this school's website was doing them more harm than good. Prospective parents would visit the site then leave with an impression that the school was old-fashioned, inefficient, and that a student's education would be haphazardly put together.

To counter this, we created a very simple and inexpensive website that covered all the basics:

- It was aimed at the only audience that mattered — prospective parents. Existing parents, students, and staff were already appropriately addressed by the school's intranet/Student Management System.
- The site's architecture (technical SEO) and on-page optimisation (content) were easily found and indexed by search engines.
- The landing page and the whole site were attractive, with specifically commissioned photography that displayed the school's true attributes.

- The navigation made it clear where to go for more information.
- There was a call to action that invited prospective parents to supply their email address for information about senior school education and the benefits of boarding.
- We developed and implemented a content schedule that regularly refreshed pages, changed the call to action, and added new articles so the site remained relevant and ranked well in major search engines.

As a result, day and boarding student populations have grown, and the school is now positioned as the premium educational institution in the region.

Insight applied

- Make your school website the home base for your brand in this digital world.
- Ensure your website is an accurate reflection of your Bold School Brand, reflecting 'who you are, what you promise, and your ability and willingness to keep that promise.'
- Use all other media to drive traffic to your website, where you can engage at a deeper level through an appropriate call to action.
- There are only two digital properties you actually own: your website and your prospect email list. All other properties — Facebook, YouTube, Google, Instagram, etc. — are all owned by others and you are subject to whatever rules they apply. In effect, you rent access to their audience. Don't build your house on rented land.

negativity

polarisation

greatness

Fear of ...

change

commitment

CHAPTER TEN

The five fears of social media

Should your school participate? What if it's just a passing fad?

Fear.

It's the ultimate four-letter word.

It holds so many of us back from finding our greatness.

Why is that?

We're great advocates for harnessing the power of social media as part of your school's marketing strategy. Yet a large percentage of schools either don't use it at all or use it badly. Often, the reason for this is fear.

Collectively, the authors of this book have spoken at many events across the globe, including education conferences. We've heard school leaders describe their experiences, challenges, and successes with social media. While some have embraced it, others say they fear it.

As in many other sectors, schools often don't get into social media because their leaders are intimidated by the technology.

Yet there's nothing to fear from social media. The schools that are seeing impressive results from their efforts will tell you exactly that.

The fact is, most Heads are not comfortable with tech they don't personally understand. There's more marketing technology and communication technology (e.g. social media) than any one person can ever know well. This is the new world; Heads need to embrace ambiguity and look at the big picture for their brand communications.

If you're suffering from analysis paralysis when it comes to social media, know this: If you continue to stay on the sidelines, your opportunity to stay top of mind with your market may fade. Each day you avoid social media is another day your competition can build momentum online.

Of course, we could talk about social media fears in a very tactical sense — being afraid to blog or being nervous about tweeting. But we're suggesting these fears are rooted in deeper, more common fears we share as humans. How can school leaders get beyond them?

Let's start by taking a closer look at the five fears of social media.

Fear of negativity

Negativity is unavoidable. People will say negative things about your brand, your school, and your people, regardless of your level of participation in the conversation.

The truth is, this is probably already happening. It's foolish to think there haven't already been nasty, negative things said about you and your school in emails, conversations, and perhaps in blogs, videos, tweets, Facebook posts, and so on.

So if it's already going on, should you just hide your head in the sand? Do you think that if you avoid the conversation, it will blow over?

How do you combat negativity?

The remedy for the fear of negativity is to accept there are people in this world who will always want to complain or say bad things, regardless of how great your school is.

Negative conversations are unregulated and unbelievably powerful. If you opt not to join the discussion online, it's not going to get any better. Denial doesn't stop the conversation.

Okay, you might say, but social media is so bleeding edge that nobody else is really out there talking about schools, right? Wrong.

The social media conversation is growing at an exponential rate.

Every day, billions of people around the world use Facebook, Instagram, Twitter, and other platforms to share their personal and community news, thoughts, and opinions.

It's unrealistic to think these billions of users don't include your students, parents, teachers, and administrators, and that nobody is talking about your school.

If you accept that even the smallest fraction of the social media ecosystem might be your target market, there's cause for concern. The conversation has been going on without you.

So what can you do?

Do what the best marketers do and start telling your story. Join in. And try to do more than just describe what you had for breakfast. Make it interesting and be yourself. You'll find there's less fear of negativity when you're actually part of the conversation.

And, perhaps just as importantly, if negative things are being said about your school brand on social media, the ability to respond in real-time to these comments is invaluable. Quickly and professionally addressing negative comments can turn negative incidents into positive outcomes.

Fear of polarisation

The second common fear can be a bit more hidden and harder to recognise. Maybe it sounds something like this: "Please accept my resignation. I don't want to belong to any club that will accept people like me as a member." So said Groucho Marx in a telegram to the now-defunct Friars Club of Beverly Hills, to which he once belonged, as recounted in his book, *Groucho and Me*.

Some of us think that if people get to know too much about us, our brand, or our school — if they get to know the 'real' us — they may no longer want anything to do with us.

This fear may drive you to present yourself as someone you're not. Perhaps you withhold your opinion or point of view. Perhaps you're just trying to blend in. Maybe you have the right intentions, but you think people will see you as a fake.

A true challenge with the fear of polarisation is that you have to accept that not everybody will like you. In our estimation, you don't want everyone to like you. Your flavour of 'like' should polarise. Perhaps some will love you and, in that thin line between love and hate, you know some will dislike you.

Religion, politics, and money. Ready to tip over some sacred cows? Where you draw the line over what you discuss online is up to you.

You must pick what you do and don't want to have an opinion about. Talking or not talking about controversial topics is your choice. But say something different. Have a point of view. Let us see how you think differently.

Don't straddle the barbed wire fence. Pick a side. It's better to be judged than it is to be ignored. Stand for something.

Social media can feel a bit like a popularity contest, but it's one of sworn allegiance rather than mild association. If you want your social media followers to be passionate about you, your school, or your brand, you must be different. Pick a side of the fence. Don't be afraid to be polarising.

How do you get through the fear of polarisation? You must first understand that people buy what they love, not what they just like. A small group of people who swear by your brand is a lot better than a larger group of people who just tolerate you. The most important thing to do for these loyal followers is to recognise and reward them.

Some people think blending in is the safe move. Staying right in the middle doesn't create any enemies. But it doesn't create any raving fans either.

Think about the top stories in the NRL. Who makes the headlines? Who sells the most jerseys? The utility players who give a B+ effort every week? No, it's the standouts. Sometimes they're the superstars, and sometimes they're the ones getting arrested, but they all play outside the bounds of 'safe', and that's what gets the media's attention.

Let's look at this differently. What do you think your prospective parents are looking for when they include your school in their search? When schools are all the same, they have to go with a boring, safe option. But what if one of the options was different? What if that school had a personality, a point of view, and a bit of swagger? Do you think that could tip the scales?

Staying in the safe and boring middle doesn't count as shaking it up. Be polarising, if only a little bit!

Fear of commitment

This fear first expresses itself as a fear of committing to a focus within your school. The most obvious example is the all too common 'we do a little bit of everything' positioning.

First of all, 'everything' isn't memorable. It can't be. Secondly, you're not taking a position that anyone can get excited about. You're straddling the barbed wire fence again. You have to assume a stance.

The fear of committing to a focus also expresses as a fear of committing to social media marketing because it appears to be a giant waste of time.

There are wasteful ways to spend time on social media so, like any other productive marketing activity, it requires a strategy. Your team needs to remember there's a difference between social networking and social *not*working.

But what if you already have a strategy? What if you commit time to social media and don't get any response? Aren't there better uses of your time? Why should you divide your focus and engage in this new media?

Why indeed.

According to Statista.com, in 2008, 100 million people were consuming content on Facebook every month. Now, Facebook is the biggest social network in the world, with nearly 2.4 billion active monthly users worldwide. In the past two years alone, it has experienced a 23 percent increase in usage.

So there are several billion reasons to engage through social media. And that's just one platform.

All the indicators show that these numbers will keep going up across multiple platforms. Social media in all its forms has reached critical mass, and it's not going away.

Of course, social media is not a silver bullet for your marketing plan. However, there's no denying that traditional intrusion marketing is dying and will soon be a thing of the past (intrusion being the act of sending unsolicited messages to an end user and expecting them to respond).

Unsolicited direct mail, untargeted email blasts, and mass telemarketing are quickly being replaced by education and entertainment strategies such as blogging, white papers, and webinars.

Why? One reason is that people are protecting their time like never before because they seem to have less and less of it, while being asked to produce more and more. An intrusion of any kind will quickly be looked at as outright criminal and, if you aren't leveraging permission strategies, you may find your school going the way of the dinosaur.

This being the case, how do you not just commit to social media, but do so successfully? It can appear complex and daunting.

The place to start is to look back at your positioning strategy:

'Who are we? What do we do? Who are we not?'

Which social networks should you pursue? Should you concentrate on more than one? Should you just do a little bit of everything, or focus?

Maybe you've heard something like this:

"I don't think our prospective parents are on social media, especially not Twitter."

That's an assumption, not a fact. Your challenge is to find out. How do you know where your prospective parents spend their time online? Ask them. Send out a survey. Or call them. Any excuse to demonstrate you're paying attention to them and want to know what they think is a great reason to touch base.

You may be surprised at what you discover.

In years past, just finding a way to easily survey people and collect the data may have seemed complicated and expensive, but with the rise of affordable (and sometimes free) email surveying tools such as SurveyMonkey, mailchimp, and the like, those excuses have been thrown out the window.

Your prospective parents are people. Some may be more fearful of social media than you are, but it doesn't hurt to ask. And while you're at it, don't just ask if they're active online, but find out where they spend their time and why.

The way to get over the fear of commitment is to understand the potential of new relationships with your target market. Social media can fundamentally change how they see you — not just as an education provider, but as a friend, partner, and ally. Your relationship can change from being an intrusive marketer to a welcome and respected advisor.

Fear of change

The next fear is perhaps the greatest for many, and the most common. It's the fear of change.

Many people fear change simply because it has caused pain in the past.

Most of imageseven's new clients arrive knowing they need to change but are deathly afraid of pulling the trigger on their own.

A prospective client came to us and boldly shared he was ready to do something different. It was time to "update our materials," he declared.

He knew he needed something new, but was scared to death. He didn't say he was scared, but his fear was palpable. Sure, he was confident about his professional abilities — as Head, he had helped to build up one of the state's largest independent high schools from nothing. But he couldn't figure out how to increase enrolments further.

The truth is, the things that helped him develop the school so far were not going to be the same things that would help him grow it to the next level, or the one beyond that.

Here's the bottom line:

What got you here isn't going to get you there!

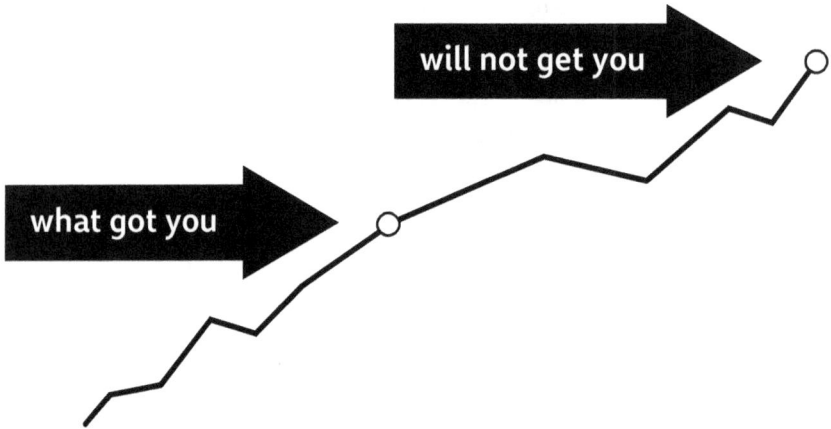

Our prospective client knew something needed to change, but the idea of completely rethinking the school's marketing approach was frightening. In fact, as it turns out, too frightening for him to green light our recommendations.

Maybe you're stuck between a rock and a hard place. You're onboard with social media, but the school leadership as a whole is reluctant to change. How can you get them off the starting line?

In the book *Switch: How to Change Things When Change is Hard*, authors Chip Heath and Dan Heath give a great explanation of how to get people past the fear of change. They break down our conscience into two parts: the elephant (emotion) and the rider (logic).

The Heaths basically argue that if the elephant is free to run wild, there isn't much the rider can do to steer or stop it. By contrast, if you can get both emotion and logic to work together (i.e. get the rider to steer the elephant), change can happen.

Interestingly enough, as people are exposed to a new concept and become emotionally charged, their first reaction is to learn everything they can about it. So that's emotion and logic working together.

Think about the last new idea or pastime you felt excited about. What was the first thing you did once you got into it? You probably looked for others who also were passionate about the topic, searched for books, and, even more likely, researched the topic online. Your passion fuelled your hunger for more information. In turn, your newfound knowledge about the topic excited you, creating even more positive emotions.

However, when you fail to find enough information to back up your emotions, they begin to fade.

Your team's interest in social media may also fade if you fail to keep them both inspired and informed. So as you get them all fired-up about using social media marketing, don't forget to provide ample information to keep them rooted in both emotion and information. Ideally, an ongoing social media strategy accompanied by regular reporting should satisfy both ends of the spectrum.

Fear of greatness

Finally, there's the fear of greatness. This may be the toughest fear you face when looking to leverage social media or any other new marketing strategy.

The fear of being great is usually tied to two fundamental questions: Are we good enough to stand in the spotlight? Do we deserve to be recognised as leaders in our field? The fear of being great is tied to your school's sense of self-worth and your confidence in its collective IP.

Do you have the stuff to stand in the spotlight?

The short answer is: Your school is probably a lot smarter collectively than it gives itself credit for.

In his book *Outliers*, Malcolm Gladwell popularised the idea that anybody who has 10,000 hours in a discipline is a comparative expert in that discipline. If you added up the hours your people have been working within their area of expertise, you might be surprised by how deep your school's expertise actually runs. The countless hours you have been doing what you do make you incredibly valuable to others.

Sharing your expertise is not narcissistic. People are looking for experts, so don't be afraid to be one.

One caveat: Social media isn't the place to scream, "I'm an EXPERT!" Be humble, and sooner or later your good work will shine through. You will connect with prospective families, convert them into fans of your school, and they will help you carry the flag. You will attract new students from everywhere, just by sharing your experience and point of view.

So, make a commitment to share your expertise and get your school ready for the spotlight!

Getting past the fears

Here are a few practical tips for pushing through each of the fears.

Negativity

Do you have negative press online? The only thing that can dominate negative content is more content. Your best bet is to start writing. Your goal should be to get some positive stories into the marketplace to demonstrate the negative stories are the exception, not the rule. Consider some of these tactics:

- Release case studies of high-profile students — past and present.
- Tell a before and after story of a student's progress.
- Highlight a parent's written or video testimonial.
- Start a blog.

Polarisation

- Are you afraid of being polarising?
- Understand that 'like' can be lethal.
- Love is a virtue. What brands do you love? Are they safe?
- Recognise and reward your core audience — make your followers feel loved in return.
- Make it easy for your parents and students to engage again and again.

Commitment

Are you worried that social media may be pulling too much attention away from other tasks? Remember, there's a difference between social networking and social notworking.

- Track your school's time on social media. See where you're getting the best return.
- Use one network to feed others, e.g. use LinkedIn to feed content to your Twitter stream and share Instagram images on Facebook and Twitter.
- Consider a social media aggregator (e.g. TweetDeck, Hootsuite, or CoTweet), so you can monitor multiple networks from one dashboard.

Change

Are you anything but a change junkie? Think about how you can:

- Cultivate emotion and inspiration. What's the most alluring element of social media? Make yourself a picture or chart to envision it daily.
- Follow the data. What metrics are most important for you to hit?
  Check them weekly.
- Plan it out. Create an actionable, complete plan with numbers, dates, and pictures.

Greatness

There's a fine line between humble and foolish. If you're still having difficulty standing up and saying something on social media:

- Count up your teachers' collective experience in hours.
- Print out that number in huge type on a piece of paper.
- Take it to your next marketing meeting.
- Commit to sharing your school's collective expertise.

Finally, think of every other fear you've conquered. What was it? The fear of heights? Darkness? Being alone? For many Heads, it's public speaking. Speaking to audiences may still not be your favourite activity, but it comes with the territory. There's only one thing that has helped you to improve: At some point you had to dive in.

You can do the same with your fear of social media. You just have to jump in and try it out.

Case study: Fear of social media can be damaging

imageseven was consulted about the best way to (a) attract more enrolment enquiries through social media and (b) create a social media presence in the community for this outer metropolitan, Year 7-12, co-ed, mid-fee day school.

The school was very conservative in almost all aspects of its operations, including its communication and marketing. Over time, it had come to rely on its position as the premium secondary education provider in the area, but this had come under attack as the metropolitan area had grown and better transport options had allowed families to consider other high-quality schooling options closer to the city. Also, competitors with lower-fee structures had improved their profiles and offerings, leaving the school well behind in their positioning.

In short, our client had the highest fees, but this wasn't supported by messaging that substantiated their preferred positioning. In addition, they had moved slowly on the social media wave.

The school had just started a social media presence when they became caught up in a media issue not of their making. Social media users expressed some very forthright opinions about the issue, some of which were targeted at the school. The issue was further fuelled by clickbait headlines in tabloid media.

The school leadership became unwilling to engage on social media because they feared negative comments.

imageseven advised on how to engage with negative online comments. However, by this stage, the school had mandated that every response had to be approved at a senior level. Unfortunately, this often took 48 hours or more, by which time it was too late to engage with the community. Being scared of negativity had held them back.

Fear of polarising the community — both internal and external — was also a factor. The school had failed to articulate what they stood for in language that could be understood by those who were not already on the inside. People didn't have a solid understanding of what the school stood for, so they also failed to understand what it did *not* stand for.

The issue passed and the school breathed a collective sigh of relief. But they lost a valuable opportunity to reposition themselves because they were afraid of change. When they moved into the social media realm, they were very conservative about taking a position for fear of offending someone. Then they were stunned into inaction because people were discussing them on social media in a negative way. Even though the school knew the full facts, its leaders let the media set the agenda.

Insight applied

- Engaging on social media (not necessarily all, but at least some) is almost mandatory for a school that wants to build a profile and position itself as contemporary.
- Sometimes you will need to react on social media as well as be proactive.
- You can't control what people say on social media, but you can control how you react to it.
- Know what your school brand stands for and what it doesn't. Articulate it in a Key Messaging Guide before you need to test it when your values are being questioned.
- As school Head, you don't have to be personally fully comfortable with your chosen social media channels. You have school marketing officers to do that for you. But you do have to set the guidelines and lead the online positioning of your Bold School Brand.
- Social media is where your parents and prospective parents are. If you are not there too in some way, it's as though you didn't even bother to turn up to the barbecue.

CHAPTER ELEVEN

Beyond the fears: Social media basics

And then it hits you: "We really should be using social media to market our school — but where do we start?"

If you've helped your school get past its fears of social media, this is a big deal. Nicely done!

Now it's time to start mapping out exactly how you plan to use social media to market your school.

Popular social networks seem to pop up out of nowhere. What, you're not using Tumblr, Viber, or Pinterest yet? While we can't cover everything that will happen in social media in the future, we can get you started with a strategy.

Remember, social media will always be in flux.

It's important to get over the feeling that you need to control social media. You will probably never feel 100 percent caught up on your various social networks. There will always be more you could do. And there will always be a new medium to explore.

So should you just give up? Not at all! You'll just have to decide as a school which networks are most important for your efforts, and which activities are most worth your time.

This means going back to your brand strategy.

Your brand strategy will help you determine where your time will be best spent online. After reviewing your Bold School Brand positioning brief, what are your gut feelings about where you should commit your resources?

Most of all, think about why you want to be active on social media. Are you recruiting teaching staff? Are you online to talk to prospective parents? Think about it.

Facebook: Is it professional enough for your school?

In the case of Facebook, it's hard to argue with the numbers. Just about everyone with an internet connection has a Facebook profile, and the number of users grows larger each day. Even so, quite a number of our clients express misgivings about using Facebook to market their school.

We think you should consider each social network and what your purpose would be for being on that particular network.

Many of our clients have individual Facebook profiles set aside for their friends and family. If they determine to 'friend' a parent, it's usually someone they've known outside the typical Head/parent relationship. We're not necessarily talking about using your personal Facebook profile to market your school. What we're talking about is having a school Facebook Page that your friends, family, suppliers, parents, and students can 'like'. When they 'like' your school's Facebook Page, your school's information should start showing up in their news feed. It's just one more way to spread the word about your school.

We recommend keeping the sales and marketing language light on Facebook. Make posts that celebrate achievements, milestones, or community activities, and posts that show a more personal side to your school. You should also consider creating Facebook Groups from your Facebook Page for your current parents, school sub-communities, and staff. This is an informal communication platform for your current community that can be made private, while your school's Facebook Page is public. Over time, you may even find that your Facebook Page is a better recruitment tool or referral source than methods you've used in the past.

Creating a Facebook Page (which you can do through Facebook Business Manager) is free. However, Facebook does provide opportunities for extremely targeted advertising within its network, even outside your friends and followers. If you only want to advertise to mothers of teenagers who live in Fremantle (WA), you can do that. Traditionally, these Facebook ads operate on a pay-per-click model, so your school only pays when someone clicks through on your ad.

Is advertising on Facebook right for every school? Absolutely not. You'll have to discuss this with your marketing team to figure out the best approach. It's hard to say if prospective parents would ever 'buy' from you on Facebook, but one thing's for sure — they're probably already on there.

Instagram: Are you insta-worthy?

Instagram is a photo and video sharing platform that's overtaking other social media to become a favourite of school marketers across the globe. Instagram accounts continue to become more visually curated, with better photography and imagery. The platform lends itself to school marketing because it's very visual and relatively quick to post on.

According to imageseven's *How schools use social media in their marketing* survey, Instagram was the number one choice for 23 percent of school marketers in 2019 — up from 6 percent in the previous year. It seems that ground has been gained at the expense of Facebook.

Just like other social networks, you can interact with other users on Instagram by following them, being followed by them, commenting, liking, tagging, and private messaging.

Being aware of visual branding is important. It's tempting to post every good-looking photo (and even an average photo can be made to look artistic using Instagram's filters), so you need to be very conscious of the story you're telling. "Look how great we are" wears thin fairly quickly. Keeping posts visually consistent with your school's visual identity style guide (fonts and colours particularly) will also make them instantly recognisable so they stand out in a crowded feed.

There's great scope for private accounts within schools. Remote families can be kept up-to-date and be included in the lives of their children who are boarding. For example, work samples and class activities can be viewed by parents from a specific class.

Instagram Stories are a particularly attractive feature for schools. They are fun and creative, with the ability to embellish photos and videos, and to link them to create a 'story'. Just like a standard Instagram feed, incorporating the school brand into Instagram Stories will help increase brand awareness and make your stories stand out from the crowd. However, the stories disappear after 24 hours, so to maintain a presence and build engagement, you need to continually provide new content.

Twitter: To tweet or not to tweet?

Are you leery about using Twitter? It's a common feeling among many professionals. And yet many professionals have flocked to this 280-character-limited social network.

Possibly the most common feeling among non-Twitter users is that everyone on Twitter is an egomaniac, tweeting some mix of what they had for lunch, which famous people they know, or how smart they are. While not everyone on Twitter behaves this way, the network has its fair share of egos. Of course, that doesn't mean you have to be one of them.

In the world of education, Twitter is mostly useful for Heads sharing links to blogs or other online content, or for following other Heads and Associations. It's also useful for following discussions beyond your normal reading.

So how do you get started?

1. Choose your handle

Visit Twitter.com to select your handle. Pick something like your name or your school's name. This handle will be your Twitter username, and your posts will show up with @ in front of them. You've probably seen this before in print ads or TV commercials. One of our authors, Brad Entwistle, is @imageseven because he heads up imageseven. You may find that your name or school name is already taken, so get creative. You'll also want to upload your photo and customise your profile page.

Add your handle as another piece of contact information on your email signature, enewsletter, blog, and website. If it makes sense, consider adding it to your print materials (e.g. business cards) and/or sharing it in articles, during presentations, and at networking events.

2. Share good stuff

One obvious use for Twitter is to share your school's ideas, links, and articles. First of all, write posts worth reading. In general, stick to what you know. This doesn't mean you have to be robotic, but if you're tweeting more about sushi than your area of expertise, some of your followers may lose interest.

Just remember this on Twitter: Aim to share, not sell. Users follow people for various reasons, but few will continue to follow school leaders who are obviously trying to 'sell' their school.

Say things worth repeating. If someone reposts what you write, it's called a retweet, or RT. If you want to share what someone else has posted, you can retweet their post. When you do so, the RT in front of their post shows you're retweeting them. When someone retweets your message, it goes to all that person's followers, which is a great way for more people to be exposed to your tweets.

If you have something private to tweet to another user, you can send a direct message (these start with a 'D'). You can also have direct messages sent to your mobile phone as text messages.

3. Grow your influence

How do you become an influential Twitter user? Start by following interesting people, or just anyone you like. Retweet good stuff. Be polite. When users tweet @ you, tweet back.

Stay on top of your account. Keep an eye on who's following you and be selective about who to follow in return — just because someone follows you, it doesn't mean you have to reciprocate. Find other users who talk about similar keywords and consider following them. Other schools, educational psychologists, education-focused authors and journalists, education websites, and other Heads are great people and organisations to follow.

Use Twitter to provide tips, links to informative articles, make announcements, share news, promote awards, and more. Don't limit your thinking to what you can fit into 280 characters. You can link to longer content such as websites, videos, and blogs too. Speaking of blogs, every blog posted by your school would be greatly complemented by a Twitter mention and link or two, wouldn't it?

When it comes to the right tone, it may be helpful to think of Twitter as being like one big cocktail party. If you wouldn't say it at a party, don't post it on Twitter.

4. But don't stop there

There are many more things you can do with Twitter. Tweeting functionality is built into various websites, smartphones, and desktop applications. There's also a free website called TweetDeck.com, which has a companion desktop and mobile app.

TweetDeck enables you to manage multiple Twitter accounts, view groups, shorten links, and post photos; it even provides support for other social networks such as Facebook and LinkedIn. If TweetDeck isn't cutting it for you, take a look at Hootsuite or one of the many iOS and Android apps built especially for tweeting.

Get into the habit of making regular updates. Choose specific days or times of the day to spend quality time on Twitter. It could be five minutes or five hours a day, depending on how Twitter best fits into your school's overall communications strategy.

Some Twitter management platforms will allow you to schedule future Twitter posts. This isn't always the best idea, because Twitter is designed to be an immediate communication medium, but it may be a good tactic for you to better utilise your time on social media.

You can also use hashtags within your tweets. This means you tag your post with the number (or pound) sign to create a hashtag, such as #boldschoolbrand. Hashtags enable other users to track tweets around specific topics. They're also popular at conferences and other events.

Commit some time to discussing your goals and strategies before jumping right in with Twitter, but don't sit back for too long. Being an active Twitter user may be one of the best ways to position your school brand as an education expert and generate leads for potential new enrolments.

And don't forget to have a little fun. If used in a balanced way, Twitter is a great way to showcase your school's culture as well as some of your personal interests.

LinkedIn: A great place to begin

If you're not yet set up on LinkedIn, it's one of the more mainstream social networks for education professionals and a good place to start your social media journey. It's a great way to position yourself and your school as thought leaders and to recruit new staff.

LinkedIn enables you to easily connect with other education professionals around the world. If you don't know someone, introduce yourself or ask another person to introduce you. Once you've connected with them, they will receive your posts in their news feed, including any articles you post or repost. You will also receive theirs.

It's worth noting that Google is rumoured to pay more attention to user profiles with 500 or more connections. The more connections you have, the more people you can impress and influence with your professional wisdom, which is good for your personal brand and your school's too.

LinkedIn is replacing the need for a professional resume, and colleagues can recommend you by writing testimonials. You can also add portfolios, presentations, blogs, and more. So it's a good place to find staff, or a job if you are looking yourself.

Be sure your school has a profile, too. You can add information and photos, and link to all your staff who are also on the network.

Lastly, LinkedIn offers premium features for paid users, including deeper analytics and the ability to post jobs, amongst other things. Although these can be useful, most users do fine with the basic free account.

Video: Putting stories in motion

If you're like most education professionals, you're probably not thrilled by the thought of making videos of yourself for the entire world to see. Unfortunately, this book is about branding and marketing, so you're going to have to get over yourself and do some video.

Even if you're an introvert and not hungry to put yourself out there, it's your personal and professional responsibility to speak up and publicly represent your school's activities and social interests. It takes some getting used to, and you won't always enjoy it. But it's the right thing to do. After all, it's not about you — it's about the school community you serve. That's what leadership is all about.

The use of online video is growing at a breakneck pace. And it's not just YouTube, although that's still the largest video aggregation site in the world. Many social networks have options for online video. For example, Vimeo, Facebook, Instagram, and LinkedIn SlideShare are all in on the video game.

So, why video? Well, some people would rather watch a 60-second video than read a few paragraphs. And, perhaps more accurately, video gives your prospective parents an opportunity to experience you and your school without ever meeting face-to-face or even picking up the phone.

If used well, video is a great way to demonstrate your thinking, show off your school buildings, introduce your team, or even show your teachers in action — literally.

But it can't be just any old video.

No boring talking head videos that reveal messy classrooms and dishevelled students. No six-minute videos telling a two-minute story. And no obviously self-serving video content.

Amateur video isn't always a bad thing, but bad amateur video can really put off the viewer and reflect badly on your brand. Goofy graphics, bad green screen people superimposed over a silly backdrop image, awkward edits, an unconvincing script — try to avoid these.

On the other hand, amateur video can work on many levels. Self-shot videos of you talking to students or staff, displayed on your school's website or Facebook page, can be cool. They help your audience feel like they're experiencing the authentic you. It feels real and personal, and doesn't have to be executed flawlessly to be successful.

Good video takes the viewer to places and tells a great story. Testimonial videos can be powerful, especially when they're showing something more than what your prospective parent can read on your website. They provide human interaction and someone they can relate to. Someone they can trust.

Maybe video isn't a good fit for everyone, but don't discount it just because it's different. Nothing humanises a school more than staff, parents, and students talking to the viewer on video.

Keeping score

How many friends, followers, fans, hearts, or likes do you need to feel successful?

Of course, that's a trick question. In the end, your numbers are just that. Numbers. It might be nice for a right-brained working environment to track its social stats, but stats alone won't yield enrolments for your school.

In reality, you may find value in tracking the number of your followers, tweets, friends, fans, or connections. It can help you determine which social networks are showing positive growth. But that alone isn't enough.

Then there are those who only want to talk about 'engagement' and 'joining in the conversation'. These terms are warm and fuzzy enough, but they drive analytical types crazy. How do you measure engagement?

In the end, the things you should be tracking are the things that drove you to use social media in the first place. If you're using it to generate new leads, track which leads have originated from, and been nurtured by, social media. If a goal was to improve recruitment, find a way to score the quality of teaching talent you find on social media versus other channels.

After all, if you don't track your social media activities in ways that are valuable to your school, how can anyone else help you determine what to do?

But wait, there's more

So are Facebook, Instagram, Twitter, LinkedIn, and YouTube the only social media sites your school should consider? Of course not. In addition to these, consider others such as Quora and Pinterest. The point is, you'll probably want to at least explore the major social networks, but go ahead and scope out alternative or additional platforms too.

Does your school need a social media policy?

Social media policies have become a hot topic for many schools. You've almost certainly seen news stories about teachers being terminated for their social media activity, former staff being sued to recover their Twitter accounts and their followers, or even disclaimers in bios featured in social media profiles. Social media policies are becoming increasingly more common and are definitely worth considering for your school.

We're no Human Resources (HR) or legal experts, but our advice is this: If your school allows or requires staff to participate in social media, having a simple, straightforward social media policy is a wise move. It's a good opportunity to spell out what's expected, what's permissible, and what activities (if any) might jeopardise a staff member's good standing within the school.

Kyle Lacy, author of *Twitter Marketing for Dummies* and *Branding Yourself*, points out that having a social media policy is not enough — you must also train your people in using it.

"If you aren't making expectations clear, it's really unfair to your employees," Kyle says. "Not having a written, communicated social networking policy is like being without HR policies."

Some final suggestions

Your school doesn't have to be on social media.

Social media is not free. It takes time and resources to maintain an effective brand presence online, and it's not for everyone. If you decide to go for it, here are some key things to remember:

- Our recommendation is to focus on Facebook and Instagram, followed at a distance by LinkedIn and Twitter.

- Set up your account for each significant social media platform as soon as you have decided on your account name, even if you don't plan to use it yet or you aren't sure. This is called defensive registration and it means no one else can claim the same name.
- Don't start then stop and leave your account with old and stale content. You will lose followers and tarnish your school brand.

Case study: Taking a holistic approach to social media

Our assignment was to build an online presence to support lead generation and brand positioning. Our client was a metropolitan, single sex, K–12, high-fee day school.

Multiple social media accounts were managed by different parts of the school. Some were very active, some were dormant.

Our first task was to audit all the social media accounts held by the school, staff, parent support groups, and alumni support group. Each account was rated for its:

- Activity
- Audience
- Impact (followers)
- Brand alignment
- Ownership proximity (owned by the school, employees or supporters)
- Sustainability

The most useful social media accounts were identified then the owners were contacted by the Head who informed them about the school's new direction and focus with social media.

Leadership was important because:

- Owners felt a sense of obligation to their audience.
- It was an expression of their personal brand as well as the school's.
- Owners needed to see the change wasn't an arbitrary mandate but part of a larger plan, where their early development work was important to the success of the whole school brand development.

All the social media accounts were either deleted, merged, taken over by the school, or given new guidelines under which to operate.

Some parent support group accounts were not included in this process because it was clear they were managed by a parent group and not the school itself. These groups were given guidance about how to ensure they were speaking in alignment with the school brand while avoiding the appearance of speaking on the school's behalf.

The process involved more than 15 social media accounts and was implemented over six months to ensure the change didn't leave a wake of resentment and distrust.

The school now has:

- An active presence on Facebook and Instagram for parents and prospective parents.
- A smaller presence on LinkedIn aimed at prospective employees.
- A Twitter account with a smaller but engaged community around professional practice in a subject area where a staff member is a nationally recognised leader.

The outcome has seen more views on the Facebook and Instagram accounts than previously, and a much more defined brand alignment in the broader social media environment.

Insight applied

- There's much emphasis in social media on techniques and tricks about how to get more views/likes/subscribers. While this is useful, for most schools it's more effective to concentrate on quality, sharable content that enhances their brand.
- imageseven's international annual survey, *How schools use social media in their marketing*, reveals there's been rapid adoption of Instagram among school marketers while, at the same time, Facebook's favour has begun to wane. That said, Facebook still commands a solid lead.
- Video, which can be used on almost any platform, continues its rise and live video is being used significantly more each year.
- School marketers believe they benefit from social media mostly through increased exposure (92 percent), increased website traffic (72 percent), and developing loyal fans (59 percent). Lead generation comes in fourth at 48 percent.
- 57 percent of school marketers are uncertain or don't believe they can measure their return on investment for social media marketing. A significant contributing factor appears to be lack of specific goals for their social media channels.

Brand culture

> A rebrand that fails to insert itself into your school's culture is sure to end badly.
>
> As we'll discuss in the coming chapters, how your team feels about your rebrand will greatly impact the success of your strategic efforts.
>
> In this section, we'll look into many aspects of how culture informs your brand, including how to roll out your rebrand, how to keep it fresh, and how your brand can assist in the war for attracting and retaining top staff.

.

CHAPTER TWELVE

Internal culture and rolling out your Bold School Brand

One of the most often overlooked elements of a branding exercise is the internal brand launch.

Let's think back here. Do you remember why most schools find it so important to rebrand?

- Hoping to shed excess baggage or negative PR?
- Need to better position yourself in the market?
- Undergoing a merger?
- Shifting your approach or business model?
- Or maybe you simply need to update your look and refresh your brand?

Without a doubt, the most successful branding exercises not only address these problems, they also serve as a compass for your school's brand.

The goal is to guarantee that everyone in your school is now speaking the same language and singing from the same songbook. Remember, branding goes far beyond the marketing campaigns you launch or open days you host. Everyone in your school contributes to the brand that your parents and students will experience.

Even HR-related problems, such as poor morale, inconsistent management, or a lack of systems, will guide how a school fully expresses its brand to the world.

So regardless of how much time, money, or effort you have spent on your rebranding effort, your team's willingness (or lack thereof) to participate at this new level and to reflect your new brand will have a direct impact on the success of your rebranding effort.

Therefore, it is essential your entire school understands what your new brand is about and why it's so important to live the brand internally and externally. When your people are out and about in the market, everything they do — the way they approach situations, treat people, and simply conduct their day-to-day activities — must consistently reflect what your brand stands for.

Your team needs to walk the talk. But they aren't going to be able to do that until they buy into, and fully understand, what the talk is all about.

The best way to get everyone on the same page regarding your new brand is to get them all involved, aware of what's happening, and why the rebrand is taking place. This doesn't mean you need to take everybody's feedback into account during the rebrand, but don't let something as extensive as a school-wide rebrand come as a complete surprise, especially to key staff and family-facing team members.

Throw a brand launch party

Assuming you're not just going to throw a surprise party to let everyone know about the rebrand, an organised party is probably the right mindset for this announcement. Choose a time and place where you can have your entire team in the same room to announce it. A branding rollout meeting should feel like a celebration, so why not make your brand launch an actual party?

The goal of the party is to rally the troops around your school's rebranding efforts. You want to create excitement and buzz internally, which will in turn spill over externally. As with any good party, plan to have entertainment, music, food, and drinks. Map out your agenda and schedule the party at the end of a work week.

It doesn't have to be overly expensive. You can host it in your school hall or (if the weather is good) in the school grounds, but special occasions call for a change of pace. How about holding it at a local hotel? Or at an outdoor park? It's really about what fits your school's brand and culture.

Let's be clear. This party isn't just about having a good time. The purpose is to boldly carve out a new direction for your school and your brand. After your team has had a chance to eat a few party pies, it's time to show them what you've been working on.

To get your message across clearly, you have three choices: Hand out a brand manual, show a video, or get up on stage and speak.

Speaking is the least expensive option, but it can be pretty stressful. It doesn't matter if you're not a great speaker as long as you get across the key messages. If you're unsure of where to go with your speech and the lead-in, here are a few recommendations.

Extend a warm welcome. Let everyone roll in on a relaxed note with music playing and food being served. Even if there is only a handful of staff, make everyone feel like a welcome guest.

Be enthusiastic. If you're not visibly excited about your new brand, how can you expect your team to be?

Keep it brief. Nobody wants to stop enjoying themselves for too long, so get to the point!

Start with a story. Tell them about how you first envisioned the brand, or what you see in the future, and how this will help all of you get there faster.

Don't dwell on the past. This isn't the time or place to say how awful the school's public perception has been up until this point or to be down on the brand's recent past. But you can talk about what you saw as opportunities and why now was the best time to make a move.

Convey the brand essence. Hit the high points and emphasise the most compelling elements of the new brand.

Show and tell. There's nothing quite like showing off your new toys — whatever you have that's visual at this point will make for some great 'oohs' and 'aahs'. Before and after comparisons are interesting as well.

Encourage everyone to live the brand. Remind your guests how important each and every one of them is to your school. Tell them how much you need them to live the brand, both at work and outside. Reassure them that they'll be hearing more in the coming weeks and give them a point person within your school to contact with any questions.

After your speech:

Distribute the swag. Once you've accepted the thunderous applause, pass out items emblazoned with your school's new identity. We've seen small schools hand out branded umbrellas and larger schools distribute branded t-shirts or hats. Whatever it is, wrapping up the event by passing out a fun item can be an incredibly valuable next move.

Let it live on. Sometimes the announcements, invitations, or press releases for your brand launch are even more important to the vibe at your party than the event itself. If you're comfortable making this a public event, be sure to hit up the right media outlets before and after the launch. Provide them with a high-resolution logo, and maybe even images of your new website and collateral.

Publicise and follow-up your launch on social media as well. Use tools like your blog and Instagram account to generate buzz.

Distribute communications documents

The information your team will receive as the weeks roll on might include a revised HR manual, updated policies, and brand standards that spell out some do's and don'ts. But will everyone in your school need a copy of your detailed brand standards manual or communication protocols? That's doubtful, so you may want to consider a lighter version that outlines the new identity without going too deeply into the marketing details.

Avoid the temptation to appear overly official with your first follow-up. Send out a thank you for attending the brand launch event or provide a link to photos from the party. The most important thing is that this next communication carries on your new look and the new brand voice.

Moving forward, you may want to give each staff member a custom-designed and branded internal documentation binder. As you issue future documentation, each piece can be put into the binder.

Initial documents to include in the binder might be:

- Mission statement
- Vision statement
- Statement of your school values and culture
- Sample elevator pitch
- Email signature standards
- Telephone and voicemail standards
- Logo, tagline, and basic brand vocabulary.

Follow-up documents might address:

- Social media policy
- HR basics
- School policies and procedures
- Customer service expectations and beliefs
- Enrolment process/parent relationship management.

It isn't necessary for every sticky note or memo to be overtly branded but remember, every touchpoint of your brand is an opportunity to build your brand equity, tear it down, or have no effect. Be intentional about each touchpoint and consider its impact. You never know who might see your branded message, spoken in your unique voice, expressing the special flavour of your brand and culture!

Case study: Tackling internal opposition to a new brand

Recently, imageseven helped a metropolitan, co-ed, K–12, low-fee day school to roll out their new Bold School Brand.

The new brand included articulation of their key messages, their value proposition, a complete overhaul of their school visual identity (logo, colours, typeface, and collateral), and a communication and marketing strategy covering the next two years.

However, the staff culture was anti-marketing, due to the mistaken belief that marketing was a form of lying.

Our challenge was to rapidly change the culture so that staff not only accepted the changes but embraced and supported the implementation.

We knew there were standard excuses for using poorly executed brand expressions. "We're not a rich school, and I've done it now, so I'll have to live with it." Or just: "Sorry, I didn't know." Of course, at its heart, these were just excuses for not bothering to make sure the branding was right, and for maintaining independence.

We decided to attack the issue head-on. The Head called an all-staff meeting with the following agenda:

- The Head explained that attracting new students and retaining existing families were key to the mission of the school, as well as being key to retaining staff employment.
- He explained why this had become an issue and why change needed to happen.
- imageseven explained the process we had gone through together and introduced school staff members who had been part of the reference group.
- imageseven showed the results of the staff survey to which they had all contributed and we had an open discussion about some key findings.
- imageseven revealed the new logo and explained how it had been arrived at. The Head spoke to how it maintained the history of the school while pointing the way forward.
- He then went on to say that the application of the new brand wasn't a negotiation; it was mandatory. He noted that, as everyone was at the meeting, no one could say they didn't know or didn't understand.

- imageseven introduced the new school 'brand police' (the School Administrator and the Office Manager), who had been given strict instructions from the Head that every piece of branded material, from a note to parents up to a new prospectus, would pass through these two people for brand approval before it was printed or photocopied. If something was done that was off-brand, it would be binned and started again, regardless of the cost.
- The Head and imageseven then answered questions together until there were no more.
- As predicted, there were only two cases where branded material was trashed. Both were relatively inexpensive photocopying projects, but the point was made, and the culture changed.
- The processes were also changed to support staff. If they followed the process, there was zero chance of a brand violation.
- When we visited the school one year later, the change was profound. Not only had the brand changed visually, but so had the attitude towards the school brand. Staff had embraced it, were now proud of their school and were showing it off to the public.

Insight applied

- The best Bold School Brand will fail if you don't change the internal culture where required.
- Clarity about expectations is vital. Many brand implementations are rolled out over time for convenience and staff can never identify a moment when things changed. So they don't change, and everything keeps getting done the same way as before.

    - Be clear about when the change will occur.
    - Be clear about who will be responsible.
    - Be clear about how the processes will change.
    - Be clear about where staff can access new brand elements (logo files, colour descriptions, and templates).
    - Be clear about what will stay the same. In most Bold School (re)Brands, much of the old culture is maintained or even enhanced — perhaps even celebrated.

- Ideally, have something that staff can immediately implement with the new brand or take away with them, such as new business cards or a car bumper sticker.

CHAPTER THIRTEEN

Keeping your Bold School Brand fresh

How to keep the excitement alive.

If I had a dollar for every client who got a little bored at some point with having a consistent brand, I'd be rich.

Maybe you've thought it before about your brand.

"We really need to add some more sizzle to our website."

"What can we do to spruce this up?"

"Let's do something different with this one!"

The exciting part of developing a new brand is that everything is new. The downside is that once you and your team experience the thrill of newness, conforming to the brand standards can seem, well, somewhat dull.

So how can you, as keeper of the brand, maintain a level of excitement while still delivering a consistent brand?

What if your Bold School Brand starts to feel stale?

Before you rush to revisit the brand, take a closer look at your brand standards manual.

Your brand standards should provide plenty of freedom to create exciting pieces while offering ample protection from doing something totally off-brand. And before you go tweaking what you've just finished, keep in mind that the only people getting bored with the consistency of your brand are probably your own team members. But you know what? Consistency and individuality were some of the most important reasons for creating this whole brand thing in the first place.

When your brand goes through rough waters, it's often more of a people management issue. Sometimes it's just a matter of keeping your team aware of what the brand is doing visually. This doesn't mean everyone should get a vote on every design element, colour, or campaign. The complete opposite is actually true. But communicating with the team is usually enough to (a) keep everyone on board with your brand and (b) keep internal boredom or dissatisfaction with your marketing materials at bay.

Sometimes it helps to point to consumer brands to convey the importance of brand consistency. Ask your team to list some of their favourite retail brands, then ask them how often these brands completely change it up. If they're being honest, they'll realise that while campaigns may come and go, successful brands are more often than not very consistent.

If you're considering trying something new for your next campaign, look at your brand standards as the ballpark you need to play within. Then find the boundaries of just how far you can push your brand's visual elements within those standards.

Does this mean you can't ever cross the line? Of course not. There should always be room for improvement. If you find your brand standards to be overly confining, here are a few areas you can experiment with.

Logo usage. Experimenting with your logo is probably the best place to begin. Sometimes just trying an alternative logo presentation, such as reversing it out of your marketing materials (making the logo white on a field of colour, pattern, or photographic background) can be a striking refresh. If your brand standards were professionally designed, chances are that logo usage isn't the best element of your standards to tweak, but if a reversed-out logo wasn't originally used, give it a try.

Colour palette. This is a good place to look next. Do you have any complementary colours selected for your brand standards? Having a few other colours to play with in your marketing materials can really open up the possibilities of what your brand can do visually. Is your colour palette too loud? Try introducing a muted colour set. And if it's feeling a little too dry, try a few pops of more intense colour.

Alternative typography. If your materials are only using one type family, choosing a complementary typeface or two can be another great way to add some variety to your brand. The first elements for which to consider new type options are headlines, body text, and other call-outs. At first pass, don't mess with the fonts in the logo, tagline, or other standard lock-ups.

Custom photography. A picture may be worth a thousand words, but if you're using the same old stock images as your competitors, or your photography is clearly amateur, it's no wonder you've lost the passion for your brand. Commercial photographers are fantastic to collaborate with. The mood, theme, or lighting of your photography are exciting elements to play with to freshen up the look of everything your brand touches.

In the end, being bored with brand consistency isn't really the best reason to update your brand. But what are some legitimate reasons why a school should look for a refresh?

The biggest reason we see is growth. However, just growing larger than you were isn't usually the only impetus. More often, growth presents itself as moving to a new location, adding a new campus, investing in extra facilities, or adding key staff.

The second biggest reason is a change of focus. Maybe you've added new offerings, moved into a new market space, or simply need to better carve out your positioning.

Does all this feel like the set-up for an all-out rebrand? No — don't have a panic attack! This framework doesn't feed on itself. The goal isn't to always be in a state of rebranding. Your goal should be to keep the brand up-to-date, unique, and appropriate to what your school is.

This means that the more thorough a job you've done on your positioning and brand standards, the greater longevity you should get from that work — and the less work you'll need to do the next time around. So instead of starting from scratch, you'll be standing on the shoulders of where your brand has already grown to.

What's next for your school?

Before you get started, spend some time on the DIY Bold School Brand audit in Section VI. Imagine your brand sometime in the future. What assets, tools, collateral, and stories would you like to have? What do you have now, and what's missing?

How can you bridge the gap between now and where that ideal brand stands in the future?

To get there, you'll need buy-in from all your school's leaders, and you may want to consider working with a brand strategy specialist.

It's important to find a branding agency that specialises in education marketing, specifically school marketing. Interview several, but don't expect any to work for free. Reputable firms shouldn't offer to do any speculative work without being compensated.

As you consider your needs, think about them like a brand strategist would. Managing and maintaining your Bold School Brand should be an ongoing activity, not a one-time event.

Building your school brand within our Bold School Brand framework isn't easy. It requires you to dig deep and make serious strategic business decisions about who you are — and who you want to be as a brand. Most importantly, this framework provides a proven process for you, and your internal and external collaborators to build a great school brand from the ground up.

CHAPTER FOURTEEN

The Art of War for talent

Attracting, identifying, and retaining talent may be the most critical challenge your school faces in the next decade.

Shots fired.

It's no secret that the next great war — the war for talent — is well underway.

It's a highly contested battle that's not showing any signs of a ceasefire in the near future.

And whether you have been working overtime to attract school talent, or doing your best not to lose staff, chances are that you are acutely aware of this conflict on a daily basis.

Let's look at the root cause of the talent war. But before that:

Apologies and many thanks, Sun Tzu.

For the title of this chapter, we owe many thanks to Sun Tzu, the attributed author of the original book, *The Art of War*. This ancient text from the fifth century BC has been an inspiration for many a business strategy, and we're not the first authors to cite the uncanny parallels between his text and the commercial world. There are an amazing number of connections between the two.

Maybe schools just suck at talent management?

Schools are simply not as good at attracting and retaining top talent as other sectors. Whether it's a far-too-traditional approach to HR, a failure to coach and groom young talent, or not articulating well enough why talented teachers should come and work at your school, this sector simply hasn't done its best.

No matter the cause, attracting and retaining the right talent is a far more challenging task for schools than simply offering competitive compensation and perks. Today's top talent are hungry for something more. They're willing to go elsewhere to satisfy this hunger, and losing a valued staff member is expensive.

As Simon Meyer, CEO of recruitment, search, and advisory firm FutureYou, told imageseven:

"Education is one of the most competitive sectors for talent in Australia. The education environments that consider the whole-of-talent equation are winning the battle for the best talent in the sector.

"These organisations are reviewing and step-changing talent acquisition, talent development, and ultimately talent retention. They have aligned their overall business strategy seamlessly with both their brand strategy and their people strategy.

"Education institutions in Australia typically spend over 55 percent of their annual budget on people. The right talent strategy is a key contributor to creating a sustained intangible capital advantage versus the competitor set.

"A key aspect of a people strategy is the Employment Value Proposition (EVP). The EVP captures the unique benefits and opportunities that exist for talent within the organisation. The leading education institutions have evolved their brand strategy to include a strong content plan around their EVP, which is projected into the talent market through digital platforms such as LinkedIn. This amplifies the school brand to attract talent from both the active and passive talent market.

"Over time, this creates a sustained advantage for leading edge schools. This can be measured in many ways, but a simple measurement is the number of followers for the institution on LinkedIn. In one Australian capital city, two schools have over 5,000 followers actively engaged and sharing EVP content about talent. All other competitors sit at under 500 followers. These two schools have taken the lead and are connecting their EVP content message with ten times the audience every week. That's a huge advantage in the war for talent."

A school's ability to attract and retain the best people is not the only thing at risk. On the talent battlefield, the struggle for culture, reputation, and future growth are all under attack.

So what if marketing could give your school an advantage in the talent war?

Arm yourself with a SWORD

Five strategies have become evident to us when it comes to recruitment. They're a mix of art and science — collectively called SWORD.

Master the art of wielding this SWORD, and your school will win the war.

S is for Strategy

Simply put, strategy is about determining a path for the future growth of your culture and school.

Or, as our friend Sun Tzu says, "Attack by strategy." How did he know in the 5th century BC what we'd be up against in our 21st century schools?

As we discussed back in chapter one, strategy is one of those words that can trip us up.

To be clear, strategy in this context is not your school's overall goal, and strategy is not your tactics. Strategy is your plan to connect the tactics to the goal.

Also attributed to Sun Tzu, this quote says it all: "Strategy without tactics is the slowest route to victory. Tactics without strategy is the noise before defeat."

At a recent Content Marketing World Conference, Kristina Halvorson (CEO and Founder of Brain Traffic) gave the example of a bear hunting for salmon in the miniature waterfall along the stream of a river.

Let's assume the bear's goals were to live a long and healthy life, and to populate the woods with more bears.

The tactic the bear used was to catch salmon with his mouth.

And his strategy was to position himself in the river in the right spot, during the right season, at the right time of day to align with the airborne salmon.

As Kristina noted, if you use the same goals and tactics, but lack the bear's strategy, you could just wind up in the middle of the woods with your mouth gaping open.

In other words, goals and tactics executed without a real strategy often fail to have the same lasting impact as a well-considered plan of action.

And for your school to properly wield strategy as a weapon in the war for talent, it will require some intentionality and consideration as to how your strategy will impact the school culture.

The impact of strategy on culture

As strategies go, developing and leveraging a remarkable culture is probably about as 'in vogue' as it gets.

It's easy to show off sabbaticals, conferences, overseas trips, and other perks as 'culture'.

But as the US-based Society for Human Resources Management (SHRM) noted in their blog: "Company culture is not about being cool or even being a best place to work. It's about being more successful. Period."

Those things — the perks, the coolness, and the awards — are by-products of an amazing culture. A school focused on winning and being more successful will naturally exude some of those other things.

HR guru Rita Barreto Craig makes special distinctions between traditions and culture, noting in one of her promotional videos: "A culture is created by the practices that you have ... something so unique and special and different it makes people want to come work for you."

And while the definition of tradition is very similar, it's about passing those things on to the next generation: "It's not a tradition if it's not practised over time. If it's not creating positivity, it's time to get rid of it."

As Deloitte pointed out in a recent report, there's a strong relationship between culture and engagement — another buzzword-worthy topic. As they noted, if culture is defined as "the way things work around here," then engagement is "the way people feel about the way things work around here." Deloitte places things like leadership, reward systems, and innovation in the culture bucket, and concepts such as recognition, meaningful work, and clear goals in the engagement category.

As SHRM puts it: "How you run meetings internally, how you share information across departments, and how you do the basics of project management — these can all be low-hanging fruit that you can address in order to start clarifying and reinforcing a culture that drives your success. People need to see the changes happening in real ways for the new culture to take root."

And these things aren't just for current staff. A strategy of building and maintaining a strong school culture and an engaged team helps to attract better-quality applicants. In the end, applicants who respond positively to an accurate picture of your school's culture are better long-term fits, because they are already aligning themselves with your demonstration of culture.

Of course, for this to happen, communicating that culture through your website and application process becomes essential.

W is for Weapons

To channel a bit of Sean Connery in *The Untouchables*, we're not questioning whether or not you're bringing "a knife to a gunfight." We're talking about the assets and tools your school has to wage a more efficient war for talent.

Or to put that in the words of Sun Tzu: "On the field of battle, the spoken word does not carry far enough: hence the institution of gongs and drums. Nor can ordinary objects be seen clearly enough: hence the institution of banners and flags ... means whereby the ears and eyes may be focused on one particular point ... thus forming a single united body."

In Sun Tzu's day (and therefore in the absence of modern messaging tactics), banners, flags, gongs, and drums were means of influencing the eyes and ears of your army. That's not so unlike the tools we still have at our disposal today. Let's explore a few of them.

The power of story

Simply put, developing a cohesive version of your school's story is one of the most universally impactful tools for use in the talent war. Your story is the culmination of your brand essence, your values, and who you are in a digestible, shareable fashion.

Some of the most memorable stories follow classic story patterns (or arcs). One famous example is 'the hero's journey', popularised by the writer and academic, Joseph Campbell. It always starts with detailing a problem in the world or a challenge at hand and identifies how the hero of the story, working through these challenges and personal transformation, can overcome and save the day. Think movie trailers ("In a world where ...") and startup pitches ("It's like Facebook for gardeners ...").

A great quote about story is from the movie *The Amazing Spider-Man*. It's the final scene and Peter Parker (aka Spider-Man) is sitting back in his high school classroom, struggling with his secret identity, and his role in the world. As Peter sits, the teacher continues: "I had a professor once who liked to tell his students that there were only ten different plots in all of fiction. Well, I'm here to tell you there's only one: Who am I?"

That's a good perspective. Shouldn't your story tell prospective staff, plainly and simply, who you are?

Brand positioning and messaging

We've spent the majority of this book talking about brand positioning and messaging, so we're not going to unpack them again. We obviously feel strongly about their power and, again, Sun Tzu seems to have figured this out long ago: "If you know your enemy and know yourself, you will not fear the outcomes of 100 battles."

Or to turn it around, if your school hasn't built a strong brand platform and brand position (who you are, how you're different, and why the world should care), good luck attracting and retaining the best talent.

So let's take inventory of just a few weapons you have in your brand armoury:

- Brand positioning
- Brand voice, tone, and essence
- Consistent use of brand standards
- Communications
- Social media
- Your website.

Your website as a weapon

As we explored in chapter nine, your website is the most powerful validation tool your school possesses. And it's not just for prospective parents, but also prospective staff.

It's essential that your website not only communicates your positioning, your story, and your difference, but also provides a platform where you can easily post new job opportunities.

As well as this, it should also demonstrate what it's like to work at your school, ideally providing visual and written evidence to support your claims.

O is for Onboarding

Onboarding is about creating simple expectations for job duties and a path for future promotions.

SHRM does a nice job of adding colour to that definition: "... also known as organisational socialisation, [onboarding] refers to the mechanism through which new employees acquire the necessary knowledge, skills, and behaviours to become effective organisational members and insiders.

"From there, organisations doing this kind of thinking about culture almost always start to focus on deeper changes related to human resources — hiring, onboarding, firing, and performance management."

In short, onboarding isn't just about what you traditionally think of — filling out forms, creating usernames and passwords, and assigning computers and classroom keys. It's about the initial transfer of culture and systems to your new ally.

What does your onboarding process cover today? Here are a few elements to consider:

- Welcome packets (a great way to share your story)
- Job descriptions and expectations
- Documented benefits
- A single digital repository for documentation
- Access to teaching materials
- Orientation tour
- Welcome meeting
- Mentor or buddy system
- Recorded and automated reminders for key dates.

R is for Recognition

It's true that not everyone enjoys the spotlight, but who doesn't enjoy being recognised for going above and beyond, or simply slogging it out just doing their job over the long haul?

Recognition is really about creating opportunities for exposure for your team, in a good way.

Finding creative ways to recognise your people can seem challenging, but it is worthwhile. And the possible solutions are as diverse as the people who work for you. While this list could be infinitely long, here are a few ideas that may inspire your own.

Social media: The innumerable opportunities to recognise your team via social media could probably make up another book but, for now, here are a few ideas.

How about a digital age take on an old-school idea? Consider posting an image of your staff member of the week/month/quarter. Give their name, title, how long they've been around, and brag about why you're recognising them.

Or instead of posting a photo of that staff member, let them take over a particular social media channel for a day or week, and allow them to post about the school through their lens.

Contribute to content marketing: We've already provided insights about content marketing in chapter eight, but this is your opportunity to leverage the smarts and experience of your best people by encouraging them to contribute to the school's thought leadership content.

Submitting for personal awards: Every market has opportunities for young professional awards, recognition of service, and media stories in local or national publications. And of course, promoting your team is a great way to promote your school.

Ongoing education: Recommending or allowing for continuing education opportunities is a good way to reinvest in staff who are already showing promise.

Attending events, outings, fundraisers, and conferences: This is probably not the best fit for your more introverted staff, but providing opportunities to attend educational and informational events is another option for rewarding outstanding team members while helping them to learn more and expand their personal networks.

D is for Differentiation

How many times have you had to answer this question from prospective parents at an open day: "Why should we choose your school?"

Imagine how much more a job-seeking, highly talented teaching professional is thinking the same thing.

As we've discussed at length, it's not only important to be able to communicate that difference, but also to ensure your internal realities and external perceptions match.

One of imageseven's clients, The Scots College, Sydney (NSW), is always looking for appropriate and sustainable ways by which to differentiate itself.

We helped them create a 49-episode series of podcasts aimed at the parents of all boys, employing the talents of veteran journalist and news anchor, Leigh Hatcher.

The *Brave Hearts Bold Minds* podcast series provided practical tools with which parents of school-age boys could engage, encourage, and challenge their sons with wisdom and compassion.

To highlight the teaching staff at the College, each episode included an interview with an educator about their area of expertise. The podcasts were designed in such a way that prospective teaching talent would see educators from the College being highlighted, trusted to have an opinion, and given the opportunity to express themselves in a public forum. As a result, the podcasts frequently come up in interviews for new positions.

You can find them online at tsc.nsw.edu.au/podcasts.

Don't be afraid to use your SWORD

As we've unpacked these five strategies, we hope you have not only found opportunities for improvement, but also thought to yourself: "Hey, we're already doing a great job with that!"

Remember — master the art and win the war!

Case study: Refreshing a successful brand

The original work in helping our client with their Bold School Brand had been very successful. Nearly a decade later, what was an exceptionally Bold School Brand has become a really well-established brand. The school has grown into and exceeded the aspirations of their existing brand.

The questions they are now posing to imageseven are: How should we change? Where can we look for change? Is change even appropriate?

It's early days, but we will work with our client to totally change the way the school brand looks and feels in the marketplace while remaining entirely within the visual identity style guide that we originally created a decade ago.

The refresh will keep all the existing visual identity conventions and, at the same time, reflect the continued aspirations of the school.

What will it look like? What difference will it make? Watch this space!

Insight applied

- Almost all requirements to freshen up a brand can be made within a professionally constructed style guide.
- For most branding professionals, limitations, restrictions, and no-go zones are just a normal part of the design process. Restrictions are not bad. They are the guidelines that keep us on course.
- Be clear about why you need the brand refresh and what you want it to do for your school.
- When you think your brand is feeling stale, your marketplace is just starting to understand and recognise your brand. Be cautious. Don't change too much or too early.

Bonus content

> If you're ready to create your own Bold School Brand, here are a few resources to explore your new obsession.

DIY Bold School Brand audit

How can you tell if your brand is due for an overhaul without spending a lot of money?

Ask yourself the following:

Positioning

- Who are you?
- What is your market?
- What is your product or service?
- What is your Unique Selling Proposition (USP)?
- What is your brand essence?
- What are your brand values?
- Describe your school culture. Does it fit your brand?
- What is your elevator pitch? Your mission? Your vision?
- Would everyone in your school describe your brand similarly?
- Are important decision-makers aware of your branding and marketing initiatives?

Voice and style

- Describe your brand voice.
- Review sample headlines.
- Review sample copy.
- Review usage. How do you use your school's name in the possessive, plural, product, service, in combination with other items, etc.?
- How do you write your school name? All capitals, title case, shorthand, or something else?

Visual identity

- Is your school's name trade marked or registered?
- Do you have a single logo or trade mark?
- Is it used consistently across your materials?

Collateral

- Round up samples of your materials — brochures, print materials, exhibition displays, advertising etc.
- Do they look like they're from the same school?
- Are any of them outdated, or formatted in an inappropriate style?
- Is your brand used consistently, following a standard set of rules?
- Are the colours consistent across various pieces?

Website

- Search performance — can your school be found online when you search for its name or what you offer?

Social media

- Are your social media sites up-to-date?
- Do they accurately reflect your brand?

Other brand exposures

Check all that apply to your school:

- Sponsorships/civic involvement/memberships
- News/PR
- External assets — speaking engagements, articles, books, blogs, etc.
- Testimonials
- Videos
- HR policies/onboarding process
- Internal systems
- Enrolment process
- Staff surveys
- Parent surveys.

Envision the future state of your professional brand

- What does your brand currently look like?
- What types of assets, tools, collateral, or stories do you want to have?
- Which of these pieces do you have now, and which are missing?
- What are the first priorities for reaching your future state?

12 reasons why school marketing is different

Let's be honest. Marketing and education are often not good friends. In fact, they usually don't play together very well at all.

The educationalists view marketing as a waste of resources that could be better spent on improving educational outcomes. Marketers, on the other hand, are prone to blow a fuse when asked to deliver a steady stream of quality enrolments with resources that are a fraction of their commercial cousins. You — as a leader — end up squarely between a rock and a hard place.

It doesn't have to be this way.

First, let's be clear about the reason for marketing your school. The long-term success (educationally, financially, socially, and spiritually) of a school is dependent solely on a sufficient intake of quality students at an acceptable cost of acquisition. It's the cold hard truth.

So, with our benchmark set, and in preparation for the critical tasks of setting your marketing goals and executing them, let's lift our eyes and survey the education marketing landscape, and why it's different from that of our commercial cousins.

1. Education marketing begins on the inside

In education marketing communication, myriad people from within your school (usually not the marketing people) will interact with parents and community — your customers. All these people need to understand your brand, live your brand, and deliver your brand every day. So the job of education marketing communication is to first market internally; to align the team and to create brand ambassadors.

2. Your school's brand is important

School brands (while not always as well-known outside their target market) are extremely important to education purchase decision-makers (aka parents). It still remains true that intensely practical criteria drive school selections (think location, price, and performance). The weighting education buyers place on the school brand drives and completes the actual purchase decision. "Can I believe in this school? Can I trust them? Will this school deliver what they promise?"

3. Education products and services are usually complex

Education products are typically complex and sophisticated. Many of the true benefits or shortcomings are not obvious. Education marketing communication needs to take the technical, the subtle, and the intricate, and make it clear, understandable, and persuasive.

4. Education markets have long purchase cycles

The education purchase cycle is a longer process, often lasting from several months to several years or more. Marketing to education purchase decision-makers requires different approaches, depending on what stage of the buying cycle your prospect is in.

5. Your education selling proposition is complex

Your education selling proposition is a sophisticated offer and must present value-based differentiated solutions that support rational buying decisions. You can get attention with gimmicks, but that won't sway the purchasing decision. Complex differences must be articulated, and the messages delivered through well-conceived and compelling communication strategies.

6. There are fewer education buyers

Potential buyers of education products are difficult to identify and expensive to reach. There is only a small market for your school. From the entire population, you must find and engage with prospective parents who have a need for education (they have children of school age), desire what your school offers, are geographically accessible, and financially able. And that's just the first set of filters. If you are a faith-based school, for example, you will require parents to support your beliefs or ethos.

7. Education is an emotional decision

Education marketing communication is not rational, it's emotional — but rational arguments are normally used to support emotional positions. Being a school Old Boy is a very clear emotional connection, but dig a little deeper and you'll find these emotional connections are associated with rational drivers, such as social aspirations and community values.

8. Your prospective parents do their research

The risk of making a bad purchasing decision is high for education buyers. Their answer is research. Forrester Research has shown that over 90 percent of purchasing decisions begin online. But buyers will usually seek the views of opinion leaders in their orbit, while also evaluating references and available statistics. It's also important to understand that they do all this work not just for personal benefit, but because they also need to 'sell' their decision to others within their family — including the student.

9. Education marketers have less research data

If you are Nestlé or Unilever, you don't put a product on the shelf until you've spent millions to know it will be successful. Very few schools enjoy that luxury. Many aspects of your product are prescribed. However, the same restrictions apply to your competition. This makes success a lot more dependent on the experience and savvy of the education marketer.

10. Education deals with more people in the process

There is usually more than one person influencing an education purchasing decision. Often, there are many. Education marketers must identify then reach multiple people across different centres of influence. This will usually mean tailoring messages to resonate with each individual's interests and concerns.

11. Personal contacts make education sales

Education marketing usually doesn't happen through tightly controlled, highly crafted communications like television commercials or other mass media. One-to-one customer relationship building, through personal interaction, demands sophisticated sales management and an educated, knowledgeable, trained enrolments team (read 'sales team') whose words and actions are aligned with school brand objectives. In the end, people make a sale, not strategies, brochures, or websites.

12. Outsiders have a significant influence in education purchase decisions

Education purchasers often look outside their immediate connections to third party influencers for opinions, insight, or referrals. Don't discount the most powerful marketing tool at your disposal — word of mouth. A positive or reassuring word from an opinion leader is worth its weight in gold.

So, how does your school's marketing and communication stack up?

Ask yourself some key questions, and be brutally honest when you answer:

1. What specific outcomes do I need from my marketing communications?
2. With our current structure, expertise, and resources, is this realistic?
3. Can I clearly articulate the brand of my school?
4. Can I differentiate my school from the direct competition? If so, how?

Key Messaging Guide

Why have a Key Messaging Guide?

A Key Messaging Guide (KMG) is a valuable tool for harnessing the power of your communications in the marketplace. It provides guidance on the appropriate messaging for correctly and consistently positioning your school. Your KMG helps your team 'speak with one voice', both internally and externally, and across all mediums.

Most schools are familiar with the use of a visual identity style guide — a manual showing exactly how and when to use the school's visual assets such as logos, typefaces, and colours. Your KMG can be thought of in a similar way, except it's the reference point for your messages — the ideas, stories, and values that constitute your Bold School Brand.

Over several decades, we have continually refined our special blend. Here's a breakdown of the fundamental components of imageseven's Key Messaging Guide.

Value proposition

Your value proposition is why families (your clients) choose you. It's the benefit — real or perceived — that differentiates you from your competition. You must be able to articulate it. We focus on answering three questions: Who, what, and why? The framework is simple, but getting it right, and making it stand out from the competition, is the hard part. If there is something truly unique about your school and your offering, then this can be built into your value proposition to strengthen the statement and emphasise what sets you apart.

Motivating brand idea

The motivating brand idea describes the idea that's at the heart of your school's purpose. It's usually expressed as a single sentence statement. It becomes the filter through which all brand-related ideas, including messaging, are clarified.

Elevator pitch

An elevator pitch is an overview of your school and its offering. The name reflects the fact that your sales pitch or school description can be delivered in the duration of an elevator ride: 30 seconds and 100 words. This high-level message is useful for first meetings, networking, and for answering those "What do you do?" questions.

Tagline

A tagline is a simple and short phrase accompanying a logo or brand that encapsulates your school's appeal or mission, and makes it more memorable. When used consistently over a long period it becomes an important component of your Bold School Brand. A tagline can also be called a slogan, strapline, or catchphrase.

Key messages

These are often considered the most useful component of the KMG by school marketing practitioners. This is because the list of key messages is the pragmatic go-to list of message components for almost every purpose.

Key messages are usually expressed as a hierarchical list of succinct core ideas about your school that need to be conveyed in every piece of marketing communication.

There would normally be more than three, but fewer than nine points. The key messages keep you on script whenever you need to construct a communication about your school.

Imagine you have time to convey just one sentence or idea about your school. That will be key message number one. Always.

Then, if you have a little more time or space, you can add in the next most important idea you want to get across about your school — key message number two. And so on.

When followed, this approach gives a consistent messaging base for your organisation that cumulatively builds your brand. It's not meant to be exclusive, and not every communication should try to carry all the key messages, or carry them all in order.

Use what is appropriate, knowing that it's a great tool to give you consistency and confidence when faced with the 'blank piece of paper' syndrome that surfaces when you need to prepare an advertisement, article, or speech.

Your story

Leaders of all organisations must be able to articulate their story. Few can. School Heads are usually better than most, but not many have a well-formulated base story from which to iterate.

One of the primary ways we make sense of our world, and our place in it, is through stories. The same is true of Bold School Brands.

Brands are the stories that unite us all in a common purpose within a school, and connect us with the people we serve. Brand stories give meaning to who we are and what we do. They are a special kind of story — they are strategic.

Far from being window-dressing, they articulate key missional drivers. Ultimately, it's your brand story that helps you answer that most fundamental of all questions: Why?

Why do you decide to make one decision and not another?

Why do your families need you?

Why is it that you are better able to meet their needs than anyone else?

Why does your logo look this way?

And, most importantly to school marketers and school Heads alike: Why would someone make that critical decision to trust their child to you and your school over your competitor?

Your 5 step social media policy checklist

Just in case you missed it, the world changed somewhere around 1997. Time was split between BG (Before Google) and after AG (After Google). In BG times, you were in control of the messages you sent to your school community.

School brands were built by long-term reputation and prospects came to you to find out information about your school. Then came Google. In AG times, the world of marketing communications has been turned on its head.

Rapid changes in technology mean we have experienced a significant transformation in how people receive, interact with, and respond to information. We're increasingly using digital technology for professional and personal purposes, challenging the traditional concept of marketing and communication in a school setting.

And while social media commentary continues to rise, many schools don't have the appropriate guidelines in place to effectively deal with potentially damaging social commentary.

These schools have scrambled to secure their social media footprint without first setting up the appropriate policies and guidelines to ensure the successful execution of their social media communication strategy.

Do I need a social media policy?

Yes. A social media policy outlines your school's expectations regarding how your employees interact with social media in your school's name. Many people naively think that the commentary and posts they make will only be read by their close circle of 'friends'. But recent history is littered with examples of employees making comments or posting images on social media that fly in the face of their employers' views.

A social media policy outlines to your employees what's acceptable and what's not. In the event there is a breach of policy, you then have grounds to enforce the policy.

So how does your social media policy stack up?

We have developed a robust social media policy checklist that can help your school manage its digital platforms, setting boundaries to ensure you get the most out of your social media tools.

5 steps for developing your social media guidelines

1. **Align your social media guidelines with existing school policies.**
    There is no need to reinvent the wheel and it's important that all school guidelines are singing from the same songbook. We reckon you'll find a bunch of existing material within your anti-bullying policy — no doubt there will be some reference to cyberbullying.

2. **Be clear about the implications of prohibited or offensive social media activity.**
    While an organisation cannot be held accountable for an employee's personal social media activity, it's important to set boundaries about the misuse of school social media or where offensive activities can have a negative effect on your school's brand. It's amazing how many people have found themselves without a job after posting less than considered comments on social media.

3. **Have a plan for how you manage negative feedback.**
    According to a report by Edison Research, 42 percent of social media users expect a response within one hour. Don't find yourself on the back foot. Be proactive. Have a plan to be able to deal with an issue within the time constraints expected by your community.

4. **Identify staff members responsible for managing your social media tools.**
    Outline who will write and post content, who will approve/moderate incoming content, and who will respond to posts — negative or positive.

5. **Develop clear content guidelines to identify what information is suitable for the public domain.**
    Will you use full names of students? Will you identify the location of student events? How will you manage the use of student and staff images? Do these guidelines align with your school's privacy policy?

There's a lot to consider, but once the building blocks are in place, you'll find that managing your social media tools on an ongoing basis is a far less daunting task.

Brand hierarchy: Clarity or chaos?

Schools get complicated as they grow.

Logos and sub-brands proliferate as new programs and services are developed, and new initiatives launched. No one is sure how effective these brands are, which ones should be supported, or when or how or if to brand a new campus, initiative, program, or service. So the proliferation continues and weak sub-brands begin to dilute the school's master brand. Unloved and uncertain of its role, it's marginalised to an appearance on the blazer pocket and business cards.

How does a school get to grips with this kind of debilitating and expensive complexity? The trigger can often be a Head's frustration with constantly explaining who the school is and its relationship to the sub-brands, often accompanied by a growing suspicion that the ballooning marketing budget is not being used effectively to drive enrolments. A branding agency is called in and they recommend a brand architecture program. So far, so good.

But this is the point at which a school must be really sure about what the problem is and what it wants to achieve.

Brand architecture and brand hierarchy are fuzzy terms

There are many definitions and most seem to coalesce around the version that asserts: "Brand architecture is the structure of brands within an organisational entity." Beyond this point, it's hard to get specificity on the subject, which unfortunately leaves it wide open to interpretation.

It has been said that "the ability to simplify means to eliminate the unnecessary so the necessary may speak." If there is a usable and useful definition of 'brand architecture' and its value in a school setting, this is it. Simplicity is at the heart of brand architecture. But all too often, it becomes nothing more than an elaborate exercise in organised complexity, a neat arrangement of logos and names in which the unnecessary is merely accommodated and the necessary is often stifled.

As with most concepts in branding, brand architecture has its roots in the consumer products industry. Makers of chocolate, cosmetics, and soft drinks have long pioneered and perfected systems and strategies for managing portfolios of brands and products aimed at micro-segments of the market. These branding systems, or architectures, can take various forms.

Some emphasise the provider brand (corporate or master brand), some create brands that have no connection to the provider, and others combine these approaches. These broad approaches have been rendered into formal constructs, or models, which are commonly referred to in the textbooks as the Branded House model or the House of Brands model.

While these models are useful enough to illustrate the broad range of relational possibilities across the entire spectrum, they are theoretical brand constructs, not ready-to-wear templates that can be applied from one school to another depending on preference. Indeed, great care is required in their use and interpretation.

The textbook House of Brands model is Procter & Gamble (P&G).

P&G is a quintessential volume-operations organisation. It specialises in serving high-volume, fast-moving consumer goods (FMCG) markets with more than 300 standardised products. They are branded and mass-marketed through low-touch distribution channels. P&G also has the significant advantage of a US$5 billion marketing budget to maintain a House of Brands model successfully.

A school has a fundamentally different kind of business model

As we said previously, the supplier-customer relationship for schools is much less transactional, often requiring individualised solutions with a high proportion of value-added services. As a result, school products are much more complex. The universe for prospective school families is also much smaller and the enrolment (sales) process is long and rigorous, often involving many people.

Schools obey a different set of branding laws

In our world, a prospective family (buyer) may identify as much with the promise of the school brand as they do with specific features of, say, a sporting program or an academic track record. No doubt price, quality, and product features will always be important factors in the buying process, but school branding will be much less effective without the presence of a strong, overarching master brand.

For Heads in multi-campus schools — particularly schools that have multiple geographic locations — the challenge can be exacerbated by tribalism, in which brands become a proxy for control and bulwarks against what's considered to be administrative interference.

It all comes down to a question of context and balance

A Bold School Brand is an essential starting point. It defines how the school makes strategic sense as a whole, a key stakeholder message, and also makes an important customer promise that underpins the performance of individual programs, campuses, or initiatives.

This kind of relationship requires a dynamic, flexible framework that's capable of inserting and deleting sub-brands as required. Call it brand architecture, call it brand hierarchy, but make sure your internal marketing talent and your external brand consultant understand the difference between business brands and school brands.

Resources

Books mentioned in *Bold School Brand*:

- Fried, J and Hansson, D. (2010). *ReWork: Change the Way You Work Forever*. London, UK: Vermilion.
- Gladwell, M. (2008). *Outliers: The Story of Success*. New York, NY: Little, Brown and Company.
- Godin, S (2005). *Purple Cow*. UK: Penguin.
- Heath, C and Heath, D. (2010). *Switch: How to Change Things When Change Is Hard*. London, UK: Random House.
- Hogshead, S. (2010). *Fascinate: Your 7 Triggers to Persuasion and Captivation*. HarperCollins Publishers.
- Kim, W and Mauborgne, R. (2005). *Blue Ocean Strategy*. Boston, MA: Harvard Business School Press.
- Lacy, K. (2011). *Twitter Marketing for Dummies*. New York, NY: John Wiley & Sons.
- Neumeier, M. (2006). *The Brand Gap: How to Bridge the Distance Between Business Strategy and Design*. Indianapolis, IN: New Riders.
- Tsu, S and Minford, J. (2009). *The Art of War*. New York, NY: Penguin Books.

Other useful books:

- Baer, J and Lemin, D. (2018). *Talk Triggers*. New York, NY: Portfolio Penguin
- Calloway, J. (2009). *Becoming a Category of One*. Hoboken, NJ: John Wiley & Sons.
- Carroll, B. (2006). *Lead Generation for the Complex Sale*. New York, NY: McGraw-Hill Education.
- Godin, S. (2018). *This is Marketing*. UK: Penguin.
- Halligan, B and Shah, D. (2014). *Inbound Marketing, Revised and Updated*. New York, NY: John Wiley & Sons.
- James J Darazsdi. (2015). *Service Fanatics: How to Build Superior Patient Experience the Cleveland Clinic Way*. McGraw-Hill Education.
- Miller, D. (2017). *Building a Story Brand*. Harper Collins Leadership.
- Pulizzi, J. (2014). *Epic Content Marketing*. New York, NY: McGraw-Hill Education.
- Rose, R and Johnson, C. (2015). *Experiences: The 7th Era of Marketing*. Cleveland, OH: Content Marketing Institute.
- Simon, C. (2016). *Impossible to Ignore*. New York, NY: McGraw-Hill Education.
- Trout, J, Rivkin, S and Ries, A. (1996). *The New Positioning*. New York, NY: McGraw-Hill Education.

About the Authors

Brad Entwistle

Brad Entwistle is the Founding Partner of education marketing firm imageseven and Editor of the *School Marketing Journal*. A prolific writer and presenter of marketing content, an insightful strategist and forward thinker, Brad has spent his entire career solving problems for clients. It is these deep insights that have earned him the reputation as the ultimate authority on all things school marketing.

Over thirty years of experience working with schools, in radio production, retail, crisis communications, and consultancy have heightened Brad's uncanny ability to analyse an issue then construct a clear and practical pathway to success. This book is the culmination of ideas that have contributed to the building of a solid brand framework that works.

Brad's lifelong passion for both the strategy and execution of marketing leave little time for anything else, but you might find him studying antique maps or watching basketball with his wife and son.

Contact Brad via imageseven.com.au or brad@imageseven.com.au

Josh Miles

Josh Miles is a brand-obsessed keynote speaker and caffeine addict focused on helping others make their creative obsessions their profession.

As a past TEDx presenter and author, Josh speaks across the US on branding and marketing, including his role hosting the podcasts *Obsessed with Design* and *PSM Show.* Josh is an advisory board member of the Purdue University Lamb School of Communication, and also consults with and is involved in several startups.

Josh previously co-founded branding agency MilesHerndon, and has served as an adjunct faculty member for three university-level graphic design programs. Josh is a past advisor to the Nfluence Network, an international church planting and resourcing organisation for churches spreading the gospel of God's grace, and the Indiana chapter of the Cystic Fibrosis Foundation.

Contact Josh via JoshMiles.com or josh@boldbrand.com

Andrew Sculthorpe

Andrew Sculthorpe (aka Scully) is the Managing Partner of imageseven, the Australian-based education marketing firm, where he takes the lead in delivering on insight and strategy. His wealth of experience has seen him public speaking around the world, publishing magazines and books, and working as an advertising director, film extra, sports coach, and lead marketing man.

Scully began his career on London's Fleet Street over thirty years ago, and his deep knowledge of content has enabled him to bring corporate level marketing and communications to the education sector. The expertise gained from working closely with clients has made him the ideal combination of marcom practitioner and business advisor, topped off with a twist of English humour.

When he's not podcasting, writing, consulting, or running a busy firm, you'll find Scully with his wife and two sons in Perth, or on a cricket oval somewhere.

Contact Andrew via imageseven.com.au or andrew@imageseven.com.au

www.ingramcontent.com/pod-product-compliance
Lightning Source LLC
Chambersburg PA
CBHW071602210326
41597CB00019B/3372